YOU'RE SOMEONE SPECIAL

Books by Bruce Narramore

Adolescence Is Not an Illness

Freedom From Guilt (coauthor)

A Guide to Child Rearing
    (workbook for *Help! I'm a Parent*)

Help! I'm a Parent

No Condemnation

An Ounce of Prevention

Parenting With Love and Limits

Why Children Misbehave

You're Someone Special

BRUCE NARRAMORE

YOU'RE SOMEONE SPECIAL

PYRANEE
BOOKS

Zondervan Publishing House
Grand Rapids, Michigan

Acknowledgments

page 13 *The Calvary Road* by Roy Hession, Christian Literature Crusade, © 1964, used by permission.

page 25 *The King of the Earth* by Erich Sauer, Paternoster Press, © 1962, used by permission.

page 28 *Why I Am Not a Christian and Other Essays on Religion and Related Subjects* by Bertrand Russell, Simon and Schuster, © 1962, used by permission.

page 29 *Genesis in Space and Time* by Francis A. Schaeffer, © 1972 by L'Abri Fellowship, InterVarsity Press.

page 104 *The Calvary Road* by Roy Hession, Christian Literature Crusade, © 1964, used by permission.

page 110 "You're Something Special," © 1974 by William J. Gaither, used by permission.

page 130 "I Am a Promise" © 1975 by William J. Gaither, used by permission.

page 135 *Systematic Theology* by A. H. Strong, Fleming H. Revell, © 1907, used by permission.

page 162 *Victory Through Surrender* by E. Stanley Jones, Abingdon Press, © 1966, used by permission.

Unless otherwise indicated, all New Testament references are taken from the Holy Bible: New International Version (North American Edition), copyright © 1978 by The International Bible Society, and used by permission of Zondervan Bible Publishers; and all Old Testament references are taken from the New American Standard Bible, © The Lockman Foundation 1960, 1962, 1963, 1968, 1971, 1972, 1973, 1975, and are used by permission.

You're Someone Special
© 1978 by The Zondervan Corporation
Grand Rapids, Michigan

Pyranee Books are published by Zondervan Publishing House, 1415 Lake Drive, S.E., Grand Rapids, Michigan 49506

Library of Congress Cataloging in Publication Data

Narramore, Bruce.
    You're someone special.

    Includes index.
    1. Christian life—1960- 2. Self-acceptance.
I. Title.
BV4501.2.N33   131'.31   78-5423
ISBN 0-310-30331-1

Printed in the United States of America

90 91 92 93 94 95 / CH / 26 25 24 23 22

To
some special people:
Dick, Alice, Bill, and Bev

Contents

You
Can Love
Yourself

1
You Can Love Yourself

A young boy posted a sign in bold letters on his bedroom wall: "I'm me and I'm good 'cause God made me and God don't make junk!" Poor grammar, perhaps, but a great attitude toward life! This boy already had a key to life that many older people never find: he had a positive attitude toward himself.

Most of us have mixed feelings about ourselves. We fluctuate between periods of relative contentment and times of self-dissatisfaction. Sometimes we like ourselves; sometimes we don't. When we feel right about ourselves, we are happy, confident, relaxed, and alert. When we don't, we become pressured, anxious, irritable, or "down."

Our attitude toward ourselves —our self-concept or our self-image—is one of the most important things we possess. Our self-concept is the source of our personal happiness or lack of it. It establishes the boundaries of our accomplishment and defines the limits of our fulfillment. If we think little of ourselves, we either accomplish little or drive ourselves unmercifully to disprove our negative self-evaluation. If we think positively about ourselves, we are free to achieve our true potential. Psychological research indicates that people with a positive self-concept are more at peace with themselves and those about them. Consequently, they are more creative, confident, and socially active than people with a low self-concept. Did you know that marital problems, worry, jealousy, outbursts of temper, overeating, "workaholism," discouragement and the inability to relax and enjoy vacations are all manifestations of a lack of self-acceptance? They are! In fact, these are just a few of the many symptoms that demonstrate the lack of a truly positive attitude toward ourselves. Let's look at some of these areas where our self-acceptance (or lack of it) makes its presence known.

You Can Love Yourself . . . and Overcome Depression

Our society is experiencing an epidemic of depression. In spite of our affluence, millions of Americans are laboring under a heavy load of discouragement and depression. At its root, depression is a lack of self-acceptance. When we get down—discouraged and depressed—we are really engaging in a process of self-rejection. We have judged ourselves or our performance and found it lacking. We have decided that we aren't worth loving. Although depression is a complex emotion involving feelings of guilt and hidden resentment, it is based on a lack of self-love or self-esteem. When we really like ourselves, we don't fall victim to self-hatred and self-rejection.

You Can Love Yourself . . . and Learn to Handle Anger

Harold has a terrible temper. He loses his cool quickly and seldom says a good word about anybody. He is critical, superior, and often holds a grudge. As one person put it, "Harold doesn't like a soul!" The truth is, Harold doesn't like himself; he has a problem with self-acceptance. Since he doesn't like himself, he is easily bent out of shape. The slightest problem upsets his entire system, and he isn't secure enough to relax and take it easy.

Gossip, outbursts of temper, criticism, and holding a grudge are all forms of anger and stem from a lack of self-acceptance. If we are at peace with ourselves, we find it easy to like others and value them as persons. We can be open, honest, and accepting. But if we inwardly dislike ourselves, we are apt to turn our criticism outward. We find faults in others to ward off our own self-criticism. As long as we are finding fault with others, we temporarily hide our dislike for ourselves.

You Can Love Yourself . . . and Resolve Your Jealousy

Jealousy is another symptom of a lack of self-acceptance. I know a woman who is inordinately jealous. She can't tolerate her husband looking at another woman. Every female is a threat and she "knows" she can't trust her husband. She grills him when he comes home late from work and is suspicious anytime he is away from home. She doesn't even trust him out of her sight at church!

This woman thinks her husband has a problem. Actually, she has the problem. Her husband loves her deeply and has never been unfaithful. But because she doesn't like herself, she cannot trust her husband's love. Many of us are a bit this way. We can't accept and trust another's love because we lack a basic sense of self-acceptance.

You Can Love Yourself . . . and Not Feel Guilty

I was a grown man before I ever heard that it was good to love myself. Well-meaning but misguided pastors and teachers had somehow communicated to me that positive attitudes about myself were wrong. In fact, I had been warned not to think too highly of myself lest I commit the sin of pride. Many people, especially Christians, have shared similar experiences with me. They have told how the concepts of humility, pride, and self-denial have been drilled into them with the result that they were afraid to think positively about themselves. We encounter this view in print also:

> Those who have been in tropical lands tell us that there is a big difference between a snake and a worm, when you attempt to strike at them. The snake rears itself up and hisses and tries to strike back—a true picture of self. But a worm offers no resistance; it allows you to do what you like with it, kick it or squash it under your heel—a picture of true brokenness. Jesus was willing to become just that for us—a worm and no man. He did so, because that is what he saw us

to be, worms having forfeited all rights by our sins, except to
deserve hell. And he now calls us to take our rightful place as
worms for him and with him.[1]

Teachings like this instill deep self-doubt and cut away at the
foundation of self-esteem. Carried to its conclusion, this concept
frustrates and defeats innumerable seekers of spiritual truth. I
believe that for far too long the church has promoted a psycholog-
ically unhealthy attitude toward the self or allowed such unhealthy notions to exist unchallenged.

You Can Love Yourself . . . and Learn to Relax

A friend of mine named Al has a common problem. Al is a
workaholic. He continually strives to get ahead. He arrives at
work early, stays late, and frequently brings jobs home in the
evening. When vacation time approaches, Al wonders if he can
afford to get away. If he does take a few days off, he plans his
vacation step by step. The first day, the family has to cover three
hundred miles and visit a certain tourist attraction. The next day,
they have to log another three hundred miles and take in another
sight. Day by day, Al structures their vacation. There is practically no time for pure relaxation. Everyone is far too busy. When
the vacation finally ends, the whole family is exhausted. They
return home worn-out and in need of another week to recuperate
from the vacation. Once again, Al has turned their vacation into
work. He could not allow himself to just sit quietly beside a
mountain stream. He had to keep doing something to avoid
becoming anxious or uneasy.

Some people believe that Al is a successful man. His family,
however, sees it differently. Al's workaholic syndrome is driving
his wife and family right up a tree. His wife wants time with her
husband and a calm vacation, and the children need a father. But
Al is so determined to carry out his plans and get ahead at the
office that everything else is secondary. For some reason, he
cannot accept himself the way he is. He has to drive himself to get
ahead. Perhaps he is trying to demonstrate his worth to his
parents or to a competitive sibling. In any case, the pressure that
accompanies his efforts reveals the truth: Al's outward dedication,

hard work, and "success" are the result of his feelings of inadequacy and self-rejection. If he really felt good about himself, he could relax and enjoy life. He wouldn't have to be constantly doing something to prove his worth.

You Can Love Yourself . . . and Not Be Perfect

Men aren't the only workaholics. Take Alice, for example. Her home is always spotless. If you arrive early for a formal dinner, she greets you at the door and everything is in order. The table is set, dinner is in the oven, the house is immaculate, and Alice is in complete control. If you just drop by, things are still in place. Alice has three children and serves on two committees at church and one at school, and onlookers wonder how she can possibly be so efficient. To them, she seems like superwoman.

But if you could look beneath her competent exterior, you would discover a different person. Alice, you see, is afraid to let her hair down and be herself. She is afraid that if she relaxes, even for a moment, people will see beneath her external perfectionism and not like what they see. Since she doesn't really accept herself, she has to work continuously to prove her worth and value.

Bea reacts differently to entertaining; she panics every time anyone comes over. Days before the company arrives, Bea's anxiety starts to mount. In order to have things come out well, she prepares everything ahead of time. Three or four days before the big event, she cleans the living room and dining room and warns the family not to use them. Two days ahead, she washes the windows and threatens the first person who lays a finger on them. The day before the party, she sets the dishes on the table. And on and on it goes. But in spite of all her preparation, Bea's anxiety and temper rise. The closer the occasion comes, the more anxious she becomes. Irritable toward her husband and the children, her temper flares at the slightest provocation. By the time the guests arrive, she is in a state of continual anxiety and tension.

For years, Bea couldn't understand why she got uptight. Then she discovered the answer. Her mother, an impeccable hostess, always had everything in complete control. She could entertain with ease and had a knack for managing large groups. Bea's father, a perfectionist, periodically criticized Bea's cooking and homemaking skills. Now, as an adult, Bea was carrying a double burden. She was comparing herself to her mother—the ideal hostess—and evaluating her performance by her father's perfectionistic standards. This combination undermined her confidence and made all entertainment a hassle. She couldn't accept herself the way she was. She couldn't entertain for fun and was unable to relax and enjoy the preparations. Living under the constant pressure of her parents' expectations made it impossible for her to accept herself.

You Can Love Yourself . . . and Improve Your Marriage

Marriage is another realm where self-acceptance plays an important part. When we don't value ourselves and our abilities, we are likely to be extremely sensitive and edgy. We interpret the slightest suggestion from our mate as harsh criticism, unwanted pressure, or persistent nagging. Whenever a difference of opinion crops up, we struggle to prove our point and defend our position in order to protect our shaky self-esteem. We become touchy, irritable, anxious, or depressed, and fail to communicate constructively. Since we aren't at peace with ourselves, all communication is threatening. Discussion becomes a forum for proving that we are right instead of a time to share mutual concerns. Sexual relations become a way of demonstrating our adequacy or fulfilling our desires, rather than a mutually gratifying experience.

These and other problems in marriage stem from our own lack of confidence, security, and self-esteem. When we aren't comfortable with ourselves, we repeatedly get caught in cycles of conflict with our mates.

As a psychologist, I have seen an interesting phenomenon take place in many marriages. One partner comes for counseling. He (or she) doesn't have a really severe marriage problem, but is unhappy and wants to work out some problems. As counseling continues, he makes occasional reference to his marital conflicts, but largely concentrates on his sense of dissatisfaction with himself. Gradually, however, as his attitude toward himself begins to change, his marriage also picks up new life. He finds himself less bothered by little problems and more able to communicate. As his wife begins to respond to his increasing sensitivity, a positive cycle is set in motion. Sometimes the change is most dramatic. As one man put it, "It's amazing how my *wife* has changed since *I've* been in counseling!"

You Can Love Yourself . . . and Grow

The people in this chapter are all suffering from essentially the same problem. They are unable or unwilling to accept themselves the way they are. This attitude—this lack of self-love or self-acceptance—is the root of many of our problems. Until we learn to accept ourselves the way we are, all our hopes for growth are doomed. We spend so much time and energy warding off negative valuations and living under pressure that we are not free to grow, develop, and fulfill our true potential. Only when we accept ourselves the way we are—with our assets and our liabilities—do we become free to become all we are meant to be. This process of self-acceptance is the message of this book.

The more I study the Bible, the more I see that every human being is entitled to an attitude of self-acceptance, self-love, and self-esteem. The Bible clearly teaches that we should love ourselves. It says that we are created in the image of God. It says that we are creatures of worth and value. And it says that we are so important that Christ sacrificed His life for us. The Bible also teaches that positive self-evaluation in no way contradicts other biblical teachings on humility and self-denial.

I am deeply concerned about the lack of self-love and self-esteem that troubles so many of us. The solution to many of our personal problems lies in a better attitude toward ourselves. If we can only learn to like ourselves, then our discouragements, hostilities, and anxieties will begin to fade. But to do this, we must have a firm foundation for our self-esteem. I believe this foundation is found in the Bible.

Notes

1. Roy Hession, *The Calvary Road* (Fort Washington, Pa.: Christian Literature Crusade, 1964), p. 15.

Foundations
for Self-
acceptance

2
Foundations for Self-acceptance

I remember the first time the idea of loving myself crossed my mind. I was talking with a group of friends and one of them stated, "Christ said that we were to 'love our neighbors as ourselves.' This," he continued, "obviously means that we should love ourselves. Why else would Christ say 'as yourself'?" Then he went on to say that Christ was really giving us a basic psychological principle—we must love ourselves before we can love another person.

In a way, I agree with my friend. It is a psychological fact that love is learned and that we must personally experience love before we can give it away to others. But his logic and biblical interpretation bothers me a bit. It seems to me that Christ's primary intent in this passage is to tell us how to love our neighbors, *not* how to love ourselves. Building a case for self-love on this verse seems highly questionable.

Since that time, I have heard many other speakers offer this view. Each time, I have the same uneasy reaction. I believe these people are right when they tell us to love ourselves. But they are wrong in trying to base self-love on this passage. In fact, I fear that many of us are taking this verse out of context and using it to "proof-text" an essentially secular view of self-love. Under the influence of humanistic psychologists like Carl Rogers and Abraham Maslow, many of us Christians have begun to see our need for self-love and self-esteem. This is a good and necessary focus. But as is so often the case, we fail to carefully evaluate a set of concepts; instead, we unthinkingly proof-text them into our Christian vocabulary. This is most unfortunate. If we understand the entire message of the Bible, we don't have to base our self-esteem on a questionable interpretation of one biblical statement. We can base it on the entire fabric of divine revelation.

From the first chapter of Genesis to the last chapter of Revelation, the Bible stresses that God places high value on man. Man's worth is emphasized throughout Scripture. In the first chapter of Genesis we are told that we are created in God's image (Gen. 1:26-27). The Book of Psalms describes us as being "crowned with glory and majesty" (Ps. 8:5). And the last chapter of Revelation tells us we will spend eternity with God (Rev. 22:1-5). These and other passages give at least seven reasons why we should love ourselves. First is the fact that God created us in His image; this is the foundation for self-love.

A Royal Heritage

While attending a meeting of scholars, Thomas Carlyle, the famous English author, was asked to express his view of man's origin and descent. "Gentlemen," he declared, "you place man a little higher than the tadpole. I hold with the ancient singer, 'thou hast made him a little lower than the angels.'"

In this simple reply, Carlyle put his finger on the problem of man's identity. Either man is an advanced animal—the highest one to date—or he is the eternal creation of the living God. Our whole identity hinges on this issue. Are we just another step in the evolutionary process, an accidental product of time plus chance? Or are we the result of the creative genius of the God of the universe? According to the Bible, we are the latter. We are created a "little lower than the angels" (Ps. 8:5 KJV).

Here is the bedrock for self-esteem. We are created by the hand of God and in His image. Just as a book reflects its author, you and I reflect a portion of God's character. We are said to be His "likeness" (Gen. 1:26). Like God, we have great intellectual capacities. We are able to amass vast amounts of knowledge and use this information to make complex decisions. Like God, we also have the capacity for self-determination. We can plan ahead, foresee results, and make major choices that affect our destiny. We also have the capacity for language and we have great creative ability. We are able to explore nature, produce new inventions and create great works of art. We can use our genius for the service of mankind.

But the image of God goes deeper still. We have a moral nature that enables us to deal with spiritual and ethical matters. God built into Adam and Eve an inherent goodness. Adam and Eve were not morally neutral computers; their moral nature was stamped into the center of their being by the hand of God. We know that God was pleased with His creation because the Book of Genesis states that He "saw all that He had made, and behold, it was very good" (Gen. 1:31).

But what about sin? Weren't we ruined and didn't we become worthless when Adam and Eve plunged our race into rebellion? Definitely not! Sin greatly corrupts our lives and mars the image of God, but it doesn't wipe it out. We are still divine creations, with intellectual abilities, a knowledge of right and wrong, the capability to make choices, and the powers of communication and creativity. While these likenesses have been damaged, they continue to exist and will be totally restored in eternity.

Even New Testament writers recognize the image of God in man. James warns against cursing other people because they are made in the likeness of God (James 3:8-10). According to Paul the Christians at Corinth were the image and glory of God (1 Cor. 11:7). This is a remarkable comment considering the condition of the church there. The Christians were quarrelsome, boastful, immature, and immoral; they were even suing each other in secular courts (1 Cor. 6:1-7). Yet, in spite of all their sins and failures, Paul never lost sight of the fact that they were the image-bearers of God. The same is true of you and me. No matter what our state in life, God sees us *in His image*.

The Culmination of Creation

The Book of Genesis records the order of creation. God started with the heavens and the earth and He formed the sun, the seas, the fish, the fowl, the beasts of the field, and everything that grows. After each was created, He pronounced it good. But after finishing the entire universe, there was something left for God to do. With all the grandeur and beauty of creation, there was still something lacking. These creations could demonstrate God's handiwork, but they could not share His thoughts and feelings. They lacked personality.

So, after all His other creative acts, God chose to create once again. This time He created man. He created us to share in His creation. He wanted us to share His thoughts and feelings, His love and friendship. We are the apex of God's creation, the culmination of His creative work. This is why the psalmist could write, "What is man, that Thou dost take thought of him? And the son of man, that Thou dost care for him? Yet Thou hast made him a little lower than God, and dost crown him with glory and majesty!" (Ps. 8:4-5). But our significance does not stop there. God didn't put Adam and Eve in the Garden and instruct them to stay out of His way. He didn't limit their potential or tell them to remain on the sidelines while He carried out the game plan. He gave them dominion over the earth.

A Kingly Calling

God placed Adam and Eve in the Garden of Eden and told them to "be fruitful and multiply, and fill the earth, and subdue it; and rule over the fish of the sea and over the birds of the sky, and over every living thing that moves on the earth" (Gen. 1:28). In the words of one commentator:

> These words plainly declare the vocation of the human race to rule. Far from being something in conflict with God, cultural achievements are an essential attribute of the nobil-

ity of man as he possessed it in Paradise. Inventions and discoveries, the sciences and the arts, refinement and ennobling, in short, the advance of the human mind, are throughout the *will of God*. They are the taking possession of the earth by the royal human race (Gen. 1:28), the performance of a commission, imposed by the Creator, by God's ennobled servants, a God-appointed ruler's service for the blessing of this earthly realm. [1]

God did not consider Adam to be ignorant or passive. God told him to name the animals and to rule aggressively over the earth. In this vocation, Adam and his descendants were gradually to bring the rest of the earth under their dominion. "God had given man a high task. He was to administer the earth in the holy service of the Most High. He was to be the Creator's viceroy in this region of His created kingdom." [2]

A Pearl of Great Price

One day while Jesus sat by the seaside, teaching, He used the pearl to illustrate what He was saying. "The kingdom of heaven is like a merchant looking for fine pearls. When he found one of great value, he went away and sold everything he had and bought it" (Matt. 13:45-46).

In Jesus' illustration, the pearl is the child of God, or, more broadly, the church of God. He chose the pearl, an object of great worth, to communicate the value He places on us. Not long after that, Jesus proved He meant what He had said. He paid the highest price—His life—to purchase us from slavery to sin. Peter puts it this way: "For you know that it was not with perishable things such as silver or gold that you were redeemed from the empty way of life handed down to you from your forefathers, but with the precious blood of Christ, a lamb without blemish or defect" (1 Peter 1:18-19).

What a foundation for self-esteem! The purchase price tells us the value of an object. Christ did not die for the animal kingdom or the vegetable kingdom. Valuable as they are, they weren't worth Christ's death. Of man alone it is said, "You were bought at a price" (1 Cor. 6:20). We are the objects of His redemption (Matt. 20:28; 1 Tim. 2:6; Rev. 5:9). What a sense of worth and value this imparts. The Son of God considers us of such value that He gave His life for us. Instead of throwing us on the junk heap when we rebelled against Him, God reached out and redeemed us.

Celestial Guardians

If this is not enough to establish solid grounds for self-acceptance, the Bible also tells us that God has angels watching over us. The psalmist David writes, "For He will give His angels charge concerning you, to guard you in all your ways. They will bear you up in their hands, lest you strike your foot against a stone" (Ps. 91:11-12). There are over 250 references to angels in the Bible. Although they don't tell us exactly what angels do for the human race, these references do make it clear that God has appointed angels to take care of us. For example, God sent an angel to shut the mouths of the lions when Daniel was thrown into their den (Dan. 6:22). Angels ministered to Jesus after He withstood Satan's temptations (Matt. 4:11). Christ said that even little children have angels watching over them (Matt. 18:1-10), and the author of Hebrews tells us that angels are "ministering spirits sent to serve those who will inherit salvation" (Heb. 1:14).

You've Got a Mansion

Shortly before Jesus was crucified, He addressed His disciples: "Do not let your hearts be troubled. Trust in God; trust also in me. There are many rooms in my Father's house; otherwise, I would have told you. I am going there to prepare a place for you. And if I go and prepare a place for you, I will come back and take you to be with me that you also may be where I am" (John 14:1-3). According to the Bible, we will live forever, and those of us who have established a personal relationship with Christ will spend eternity in heaven. After all the conflicts of the ages are past, God's eternal purpose will be fulfilled. Man, created in God's image to glorify Him and to receive His love and fellowship, will be restored to his original perfection. Transformed into God's image, we will spend eternity in fellowship with Him (1 Cor. 15:51-58).

You Are "Worth Your Salt"

By this time, the biblical perspective on our value and significance to God should be abundantly clear. God has placed a high value on mankind. He created us in His image and crowned us with glory and honor. He gave us dominion over the earth. He died to purchase us out of slavery to sin. He prepared a place for us in eternity. And He assigns angels to watch over us. If any doubt about our worth remains, the words of Christ Himself should affirm our value.

Throughout His earthly life, Christ consistently affirmed the value, importance, and worth of every person. He said: "You are the salt of the earth" (Matt. 5:13). "You are the light of the world" (Matt. 5:14). "Look at the birds of the air; they do not sow or reap or store away in barns, and yet your heavenly Father feeds them. *Are you not much more valuable than they?*" [italics added] (Matt. 6:26).

Over and over again, Christ proclaimed our value. Perhaps the best picture of Christ's attitude toward us is given in one of His final prayers to God the Father. We encounter this moving scene in John 17:9-11,22,23. Christ, facing death, expressed His deep desire that the Father protect and help His followers:

> I pray for them . . . for they are yours. All I have is yours, and all you have is mine. And glory has come to me through them. I will remain in the world no longer, but they are still in the world. . . . I have given them the glory that you gave me, that they may be one as we are one: I in them and you in me. May they be brought to complete unity to let the world know that you sent me and have *loved them even as you have loved me* [italics added].

Jesus, under tremendous pressure, asked God the Father to help us. He said that He gave us His glory. He expressed His desire to be united with us for eternity. And He closed His prayer by saying that God loves us as much as He loves His own Son.

False Hopes

These biblical principles are in stark contrast to secular theories of the worth of man. Without this understanding of our divine origins and eternal worth, it is impossible to build a reliable sense of self-esteem. Any view of life that doesn't take God into consideration is extremely shaky. How can we say that we are entitled to a deep sense of self-love and self-respect if we are simply one more member of the animal kingdom?

The currently popular theory of behaviorism is a good example here. While many behavioristic principles are workable and valid, behaviorism carried to its logical conclusion as a philosophy of life undermines our self-esteem. To the radical behaviorist, man is a completely determined animal. He has no significant origin, no capacity for free will, and no destiny beyond the grave.

In a slightly different way, humanistic psychologies carried to their logical conclusion also undermine our self-esteem. Although humanistic psychologists rightly stress our dignity and worth, they have no ultimate basis on which to build their views. If mankind has no divine origin, no eternal destiny, and no special purpose or significance, then it is *not* logical to say that we should hold ourselves in high esteem. In fact, the opposite is true. If the secular humanist's view of human nature is true, he can only be led to depression and despair. The great humanistic philosopher, Bertrand Russell, saw where his viewpoint led.

> That man is the product of causes which had no prevision of the end they were achieving; that his origin, his growth, his hopes and fears, his loves and his beliefs, are but the outcome of accidental collocations of atoms; that no fire, no heroism, no intensity of thought and feeling can preserve an individual life beyond the grave; that all the labor of all the ages, all the devotion, all the noonday brightness of human genius are destined to extinction in the vast death of the solar system, and that the whole temple of man's achievement must inevitably be buried beneath the debris of a universe in ruins—all these things, if not quite beyond dispute, are yet so nearly certain that no philosophy which rejects them can hope to stand. Only within the scaffolding of these truths, only on the firm foundation of unyielding despair can the soul's habitation henceforth be safely built.[3]

This pessimism, the logical outgrowth of humanism and the rejection of the biblical view of man, robs us of all dignity, worth, and value, and tears at the foundation of our hopes and optimism.

Firm Foundations

Compared to these secular perspectives, the Christian view of self-esteem is in a category by itself. It alone elevates man above the animals. It alone speaks satisfactorily to man's origin and destiny. And it alone provides a solid foundation on which to build self-esteem. The biblical view of man acknowledges our sins and failures, but it doesn't demean our deepest significance as creations of the living God.

As Francis Schaeffer puts it:

> For twentieth century man this phrase, *the image of God*, is as important as anything in Scripture, because men today can no longer answer that crucial question, "Who am I?" In his own naturalistic theories, with the uniformity of cause and effect in a closed system with an evolutionary concept of a mechanical, chance parade from the atom to man, *man has lost his unique identity* [italics added]. . . . In contrast, I stand in the flow of history. I know *my* origin. My lineage is longer than the Queen of England. It does not start with the Battle of Hastings. It does not start with the beginnings of good families, wherever or whenever they lived. As I look at myself in the flow of space-time reality, I see my origin in Adam and in God's creating man in His own image.[4]

This is the ultimate source of personal esteem and the foundation for a biblical concept of self-love. Because we are created in the image of God, we possess great worth, significance, and value. We are loved by God and deserving of the love of ourselves and others.

Notes

1. Erich Sauer, *The King of the Earth* (Exeter, U. K.: Paternoster, 1962), p. 81.
2. Ibid., p. 92.
3. Bertrand Russell, "A Free Man's Worship," *Why I Am Not a Christian and Other Essays on Religion and Related Subjects*, ed. P. Edwards (New York: Simon and Schuster, 1956), p. 107.
4. Francis Schaeffer, *Genesis in Space and Time* (Downers Grove, Ill.: Inter-Varsity, 1972), pp. 48, 53-54.

Self-love: Vice or Virtue?

3
Self-love: Vice or Virtue?

Nearly every time I present the biblical foundation for self-love, someone asks, "But what about the sin of pride? Doesn't the Bible teach us that we can love ourselves too much?"

This question deserves a careful answer, since the Bible does call pride a sin. "Pride goes before destruction, and a haughty spirit before stumbling" (Prov. 16:18). "Before destruction the heart of man is haughty, but humility goes before honor" (Prov. 18:12). These and similar verses cause some of us to shy away from positive attitudes toward ourselves. As one man put it, "I would be afraid to feel good about myself. God might put me in my place!" This man, a minister in an active, growing church, confused self-esteem with pride. He thought that to like himself was being haughty. Many of us could make the same statement. We have somehow been taught that a positive self-evaluation is not consistent with a Christian way of life. In fact, some of us have even been told that self-acceptance undermines the virtue of humility. Fortunately, neither of these are true. Although a number of Scripture passages demonstrate God's concern with the overestimation of ourselves, both the Bible and personal experience tell us there are vast differences between destructive pride and constructive self-love or self-esteem. Let's take a look at some of these distinctions.

Self-love Is Not Superiority

Not far from where our family lives is a church that sets just off a busy freeway. A large sign on the building reads: "Southern California's Largest Bus Ministry." Every time I drive by, I am a little puzzled. I know absolutely nothing about that church. I don't know if it is liberal or conservative or if it is a friendly or unfriendly church. All I know is that it claims to have Southern California's largest bus ministry. Of course I don't have anything against buses—even church buses—but something about that sign bothers me. Apparently someone in that church feels a need to elevate his church above all the other churches in Southern California, for the sign implies that all other churches have smaller bus ministries. In other words, this church's bus ministry is "superior." This placing of one's self over others in an attitude of superiority is a prime example of the sin of pride.

We all know a few people who have a "big ego." They may be overbearing and arrogant, or they may give the impression they are a little better than everyone else. Their "superiority" may relate to financial resources, appearance, athletic ability, professional position, status in society, or even Christian experience and responsibilities. Most of us even know a few people who are proud of being humble! No matter what they are proud of, their attitude of superiority makes the rest of us a bit uncomfortable. They stir up feelings of inferiority and anxiety, and sometimes anger and resentment.

We often say such a person has a "big head," that he is "too big for his britches," or, in adolescent language, that he "thinks he's hot stuff." Actually the person with an apparently "big ego" doesn't have a good attitude about himself. Superiority is a far cry from self-esteem. In fact, if we could see beneath his proud exterior, we would find a frightened person with feelings of inadequacy. Such a person feels so weak or helpless that he spends a lifetime building up a false image of himself in an attempt to cover up his weakness.

One successful businessman I counseled was just this way. Everyone believed that he really had it made. He walked confidently into meetings with corporate executives, had a large income, owned a home in an exclusive neighborhood, and seemed to feel superior to others. He had a confident, successful, and superior air. But when business and family problems upset his comfortable image, he had to seek counseling. His wife saw through his confident exterior and his inability to relax and be a real person. She grew tired of coexisting in a relationship devoid of love and warmth and decided to move out. That was a tremendous blow to his esteem.

This man began to dig into his problems. Gradually, over a period of months, he began to see the truth about himself. During a therapy session, he looked me straight in the eye and said, "Bruce, I'm a farce. Everybody thinks I've got it all together. Actually I feel like a frightened little kid. I don't know how to love my wife. I don't know how to get close to anyone at work. I'm lonely and depressed inside and I feel like a complete failure." Like many of us, he had been trying to hide his lack of self-acceptance behind a facade of superiority.

The word *superiority* is just what the Bible means by pride (1 Cor. 4:6,18,19; 5:2; 8:1; 13:4). In fact, the Greek words for pride in the New Testament literally mean "puffed up," "inflated," or "haughty" and communicate a proud and arrogant estimation of oneself in relation to others. This elevation of self above others is in direct opposition to the biblical concept of humility. In his famous love chapter, Paul writes that genuine love is not "puffed up" (1 Cor. 13:4 KJV). That is, biblical self-love is not haughty or proud. Such attitudes are hollow substitutes for genuine self-acceptance.

Self-love Is Not Self-will

Just like a two-year-old who always wants his own way, some adults have a tremendous problem with their wills. Urged on by their need to demonstrate their adequacy, they continually fight to have their way. In a business meeting, they become upset if a policy they want doesn't pass. On a date or an evening out, they become angry if others don't want to go where they want to go. In marriage—well—the need to have one's way can be disastrous. A husband may always have to be in the right. The family has to go where he wants to go when he wants to go. And they have to do things *his* way, since his way is the right way. Some men even use the biblical concept of the man as head of the family to justify their stubborn, self-willed style of living. This is another indication of a lack of self-esteem or self-acceptance.

We should not confuse stubborn self-will with self-love or self-esteem. The truly confident and secure person doesn't always have to have his way. He can be sensitive and flexible, bending to the needs and feelings of those around him. A true leader in the church, according to Paul, is not self-willed (Titus 1:7). He is knowledgeable, capable of teaching, and not afraid to refute false teachers. But he carries out his duties in a sensible, hospitable, and loving way (Titus 1:8-9). People with a good self-concept are able to be assertive and communicate their perspective without needing to stubbornly insist on their own way.

Self-love Is Not Self-centeredness

Every infant goes through a stage when he loves only himself. As far as he is concerned, he is the center of the world. Everyone caters to his needs. If he is dirty, someone changes him. If he is hungry, someone feeds him. If he is thirsty, someone gives him a drink. The entire world revolves around his needs. In fact, during his first few weeks of life, the infant is unaware of any world outside himself. His perceptual apparatus and central nervous system have not developed to the point that he can differentiate between himself and his mother. To him, the world is a mass of perceptions and he is at its center.

Unfortunately, some people never outgrow this stage. Even as adults, they still do everything possible to remain at the center of their world. Some of these people spend many hours in front of their mirror, grooming themselves and admiring their body. They go on body-building and beautifying kicks—not with a normal, healthy desire to take good care of themselves, but with the desire to exhibit themselves in order to gain attention. Others live a self-centered life that excludes other people or uses them only as a means to gain their own selfish gratification. When life doesn't go their way, they quickly become upset, hurt, or angry. Others have to be constantly in the limelight, always competing for status. They may even use religion to meet their selfish needs.

Paul warned against this when he wrote that some people "preach Christ out of selfish ambition, not sincerely . . ." (Phil. 1:17). Paul was saying that under the guise of Christian witness, some people seeking attention were preaching from false motives. Such attention-seeking is not mature self-love. It is a sad symptom of a lack of self-esteem. People who feel good about themselves do not need to cling to narcissistic or childish forms of "love."

Self-love Is Self-esteem

Leviticus 19 tells us how God gave the nation of Israel principles for living and worship. Spoken through Moses, these principles of instruction came during the critical period immediately following Israel's four hundred years of Egyptian bondage.

Moses' speech is the first of five biblical passages that instruct us to "love your neighbor as yourself" (Lev. 19:18). The other four passages are Mark 12:31; Romans 13:9; Galatians 5:14; and James 2:8. These New Testament passages shed important light on the meaning of self-love. In each, the Greek word *agapaō* is used to depict the type of love we should have for our neighbors and ourselves. This verb, and its well-known noun form, *agapē*, are used throughout the New Testament to describe a certain type of love. It is the word used to describe both God the Father's love for Christ (John 17:26) and His love for the human race (John 3:16; Rom. 5:8).

In contrast to the Greek word *phileō*, which implies ardent affection or a love characterized by fiery impulse, *agapē* has the flavor of esteem and regard.[1] For example, Christ used the word *agapē* when He asked Peter, "Do you love me?" A paraphrase of what Christ was asking Peter would read: "Simon, do you esteem me?" *Agapē*, then, focuses on a person's value and significance. It is not an emotional, ecstatic adoration, nor is it the feeling we have when we "fall in love." It certainly is not an erotic feeling. Instead, agape love is a deep attitude of esteem and respect. This is the basic meaning of biblical self-love. It is a valuing or esteeming of ourselves as significant individuals.

Self-love Is Seeing Ourselves As Image-bearers

When God said, "Let Us make man in Our image" (Gen. 1:26), He once and for all provided a basis for human dignity, worth, and value. He sealed forever the fact that every person who walked this earth would have the right to see himself as a creature of worth, value, and importance. This is another aspect of biblical self-love. No matter how deeply sin mars our image, one fact remains: we are in His image.

The Book of Genesis establishes that the most basic thing about us is our worth and value. Long before sin entered our lives, God designed and built into the fabric of our being a host of attributes. He created us in His image and gave us the ability to reason, feel, love and choose. Only later did sin come into the picture. Sin is never portrayed in Scripture as the essential characteristic of the human personality. On the contrary, the Bible describes sin as an intruder into human nature. It is a foreigner—uninvited by the Creator—and it will eventually be totally eliminated from our personalities. Because it is a foreigner or intruder, sin cannot serve as the basis for our identity.

Though sin will continue to exert a powerful influence until we reach eternity, it is important to remember that our sinfulness is not the foundation of our self-esteem. Our identity begins with the fact that we are image-bearers. Only secondarily do we have to account for the sin that entered man's perfect state. This point is exceedingly important. As we erect a basis for our identity, we can look at one of two conditions. We can either look first at our sinfulness and erect a basically negative self-image, or we can look first to our divine origin and destiny and then build an essentially positive self-concept.

Unfortunately, some well-meaning but misguided pastors,

parents, and teachers subtly (and sometimes not so subtly) imply that sin is the basic element of our nature and that it forms the foundation of our identity. They so frequently remind us of our failures and our sinfulness that we get a twisted self-concept. Having heard sermon after sermon on our sinfulness or received much criticism from our parents, some of us have come to believe that sin is the most basic thing about us. Whatever good traits and characteristics we possess seem entirely secondary—something added on or decorative, but certainly not an integral part of our "real" personality. In fact, our good qualities may seem foreign, distant, or accidental. This position is totally unbiblical.

Paul writes that he delighted after the will of God in his inner man, but that another law warred against this deep desire (Rom. 7:22-23). His inner man, the deepest and most basic part of his self, wanted to follow God, but sin prevented this.

Because our sinful desires are sometimes strong, we tend to think that they reflect our real self—the most basic portion of our created nature. But this false concept is not the entire story— even when our sinful desires overwhelm us and get us into serious trouble.

Underneath all our sin, temptation, and confusion, the image of God exists in man. Underneath our sinful surface, we have an awareness of our failures and a desire to do better. No matter how far we fall short, the image of God in us will triumph. The potential is there and it will eventually be developed. Paul puts it this way: "Being confident of this, that he who began a good work in you will carry it on to completion until the day of Christ Jesus" (Phil. 1:6). Although our progress here on earth is often slow, when we begin our life in eternity, we will be totally restored to our original condition. In the meantime, we are moving in that direction. We must base our principles of self-esteem on this most basic aspect of our nature. Only in the fact that we are God's creations do we have a solid basis for self-acceptance and self-love. Once we have this foundation solidly in place, we can take a look at the extent of our sinfulness and our shortcomings. We do this in order to see our need for growth and grace, however, and not as a measure of our worth or value.

**Self-love Is Valuing Ourselves As Equally
Important Members of Mankind**

One Friday evening, my wife and I were visiting with some
Christian friends. The conversation turned to the church as the
body of Christ and our individual roles in the total ministry of the
church. As we began to discuss 1 Corinthians 12:12-31, which
says that each person has a different function in the body of
Christ, we decided to go around the circle and see what role each
of us fulfilled.

We quickly agreed that Bill would be a good mouth. He was
never at a loss for words. Fran would make a good foot. Energetic
and lively, she was always on the go. Sandy, we decided, would
make a great ear. Many people came to her to "get things off their
chest" because she knew how to be a sympathetic listener.

Finally we had gone around the circle, except for Bea, who sat
quietly in her chair. A shy yet talented person, Bea lacked self-
confidence. "O.K. Bea," someone said, "what part do you think
you play?"

"I don't know," Bea replied. Then, thinking hard, she finally
replied, "I guess I'm just a little toe."

We all laughed and then joked a bit about the value of a toe. "It
gives the toenail a place to stay," Bill suggested quickly. "You
couldn't count beyond eighteen without it," another added. Then
our discussion grew more serious. While we didn't fully understand what they might be, we all knew that God had His reasons
for creating little toes. They, too, have an important function for
the body. Paul emphasized this unity of parts when he writes:

> The body is a unit, though it is made up of many parts; and
> though all its parts are many, they form one body. So it is
> with Christ. . . . The eye cannot say to the hand, "I don't
> need you!" And the head cannot say to the feet, "I don't need
> you!" On the contrary, those parts of the body that seem to
> be weaker are indispensable, and the parts that we think are
> less honorable we treat with special honor. And the parts
> that are unpresentable are treated with special modesty,
> while our presentable parts need no special treatment. But
> God has combined the members of the body and has given
> greater honor to the parts that lacked it, so that there should

be no division in the body, but that its parts should have
equal concern for each other. If one part suffers, every part
suffers with it; if one part is honored, every part rejoices with
it (1 Cor. 12:12, 21-26).

Paul goes on to list different parts that make up the body of
Christ. He mentions apostles, teachers, miracle workers, help-
ers, and administrators. No one is omitted from his list; it includes
everyone. While we may not all be teachers or evangelists, we all
can help and love. Some of us work behind-the-scenes, organiz-
ing and loving in a way that is not so visible. Others carry on more
public ministries.

Just as God used different people with different gifts throughout the Bible, He is using each of us today in a special way. We
have all been created with a unique personality and with talents,
and we must recognize that our uniqueness to God is a source of
self-esteem. We have each been chosen to fulfill an aspect of His
ministry, and so we do not need to compete with others around us
to prove our worth. As Christians, we have an important contribution to make to God's ministry. As human beings, we should
see one another as equally valuable and important members of
the human race, learning to love ourselves as we recognize our
individual and corporate place within our society and our world.

Self-love Is Seeing Ourselves As Objects
of Divine Love

Shortly before Christ was crucified, He spoke to His disciples
about the trouble and persecution they were going to face. He
began by assuring them of His love. "As the Father has loved me,
so have I loved you. Now remain in my love" (John 15:9).

In other words, Christ said that He loves us in the same way
that the Father loves Him. Think of the depth of that love! Jesus
Christ actually loves us as much as God the Father loves Him.
Following this assurance, Christ commanded His disciples to
love each other, even to the point of dying for each other.

Throughout the Bible, we are told how much God loves us.
This is an ingredient in biblical self-love. We need to learn to see
ourselves as the objects of divine love. Once we accept the fact

that God loved us so much that He sent Christ to die for us, it is much easier to learn to love ourselves.

Pride: the Antithesis of Self-esteem

The Book of Jeremiah gives us an excellent description of the sin of pride and helps us understand the difference between self-love and sinful pride. The descendants of Moab, a second-generation offspring of Lot's incestuous relationship with his oldest daughter, had become very sinful and God commissioned the prophet Jeremiah to bring them word of His coming judgment.

Jeremiah obeyed God and began his strong prophetic indictment of the Moabites. He lists three aspects of their sinful pride: "For because of your *trust in your own achievements and treasures* [italics added], even you yourself will be captured" (48:7). "He [the Moabites] has become *arrogant toward the LORD* [italics added]; so Moab will wallow in his vomit, and he also will become a laughingstock" (48:26). "Now was not Israel a laughingstock to you? Or was he caught among thieves? For each time you speak about him you shake *your head in scorn*" (48:27). Jeremiah summarized their chief sin in one simple sentence. "We have heard of the pride of Moab—he *is* very proud" (48:29).

The Moabites' pride, then, involved three sinful attitudes. Breaking down these attitudes brings the meaning of pride into perspective. Their pride consisted of: (1) trust in their own accomplishments and treasures; (2) arrogance toward God; and (3) scorn toward Israel.

Likewise, in our own lives, pride is a three-pronged attitude. Toward ourselves, the proud attitude is self-sufficiency. The proud person thinks he can rely entirely on himself. He trusts in his own accomplishments and assets while denying his need of others. Toward God, the proud attitude is one of arrogance. Based on an overestimation of his abilities, the proud person denies his need of God. To him, God is but a crutch for weak people who are forced to admit failure. Toward others, the proud person's attitude is one of scorn. Just as the Moabites looked down their noses at Israel, the proud person minimizes the value and significance of other people.

Understanding the biblical use of pride helps to clarify the difference between the sin of pride and the experience of biblical self-love. Pride lifts us above others; biblical self-love views all men as equals. Pride is stubborn and self-willed; biblical self-love shares, gives, and remains flexible. Pride places self at the center of the world; biblical self-love puts God at the center and recognizes that we are the objects of His love. The following chart summarizes biblical self-love.

Biblical Self-love	
Is Not	**Is**
1. An attitude of superiority.	1. Valuing ourselves as equally important members of God's creation.
2. Self-will.	2. Seeing ourselves as image-bearers.
3. Self-centeredness.	3. Seeing ourselves as objects of divine love.

Notes

1. A. R. Faussett, *Faussett's Bible Dictionary* (Grand Rapids: Zondervan, 1949), p. 439.

Jesus Had
an Ego, Too!

4

Jesus Had an Ego, Too!

I have addressed many Christian groups on the topic of self-love and self-esteem. At the beginning of one of these meetings, I asked everyone present to write down what they thought the Bible had to say about "ego." Then I asked them to write down what the Bible says we are to do with our ego. Here are a few of their replies:

- "Your ego is your self, the old man, the real you. It is your bent to sinning and you should put it to death, crucify it so Christ can have control."
- "It is our self, our natural man, our flesh."
- "It is that part of you that seeks gratification."
- "Ego is the selfish part of us. We should die to self."

Running throughout these replies is the implication that the ego is something evil. It should be "overcome," "crucified," "denied," "taken off the throne of our lives," or in some way eliminated. This makes the whole idea of self-love seem terribly wrong and un-Christian. If the self is evil and needs to be overcome, why are we spending time trying to learn to love ourselves?

Throughout this book, we will be talking about our "self-concept" and "self-image." When I use these terms I am referring to the basic set of attitudes that make up our total personhood. *Self* and *ego*, in turn, are synonyms for this concept of the total person. When we talk about "self-love" or "self-esteem," we will be referring to a basic valuation of this self or ego—in the biblical sense of these terms—not to a distorted view that sees the ego as something that needs to be crucified, destroyed, or overcome. Although the latter idea is extremely common among Christians today, it is neither accurate nor biblical. The Bible never says that our ego is bad and needs to be put out of operation.

The Greek word that is transliterated "ego"[1] simply means "I." Used over three hundred times in the New Testament,[2] it means nothing more or less than "I." It is used by Christ, John the Baptist, Luke, John, and Paul, and has absolutely no negative connotation.

Jesus, for example, speaks of Himself in this way. During His Sermon on the Mount, He said, "But I [Greek, "ego"] tell you, Love your enemies and pray for those who persecute you" (Matt. 5:44). Jesus had an ego too! Jesus not only had an ego; He was an ego. Unfortunately, we have so abused the meaning of this word that it sounds almost blasphemous to speak of Jesus having an ego. But He did. And so did the apostles Paul, John, Peter, and all of the disciples. Later we will look at the school of thought that belittles the concept of ego and suggests that it should be crucified or denied. But for now, we will stop with the following clarification. According to the Bible, the ego is not something evil that is to be put away, denied, or crucified. It is simply a designation for the entire person.

The word *self* in the New Testament is used in much the same way. The Greek word for "self," *automatos*, simply means "of oneself."[3] It is used in such passages as Mark 4:28 and Acts 12:10. Like *ego*, *self* has no innate negative implications. It is simply a designation for the entire person. Similarly, "self" in reflexive pronouns like *myself*, *thyself*, and *himself* refers to the whole person.[4] It is used in passages such as Luke 6:42, John 18:18, and Romans 8:16.

Since some people have distorted the meaning of these words to promote an unhealthy picture of self-esteem and self-acceptance, we need to mark the biblical design. Ego and self are not portrayed by God as evil, corrupted aspects of our lives that must be eliminated. They refer to our total person, created in God's likeness and destined to spend eternity with Him. Our everyday use of the term *ego* to refer to proud people should not be confused with the biblical concept of the whole person.

The Ego and the Flesh

In contrast to ego and self, the Greek word *sarx* is used in a negative sense in Scripture when it is applied to our style of living. Generally translated "flesh" in the New Testament, *sarx* has several different meanings. Sometimes it refers to physical flesh. Sometimes it denotes the total person. When used in a specifically spiritual sense, *flesh* represents the seat of sin in man.[5]

According to the Bible, then, the flesh is our rebellious disposition—our tendency to run our lives our own way apart from God.

> The acts of the sinful nature are obvious: sexual immorality, impurity and debauchery; idolatry and witchcraft; hatred, discord, jealousy, fits of rage, selfish ambition, dissensions, factions and envy; drunkenness, orgies, and the like. I warn you, as I did before, that those who live like this will not inherit the kingdom of God (Gal. 5:19-21).

"Flesh" is the basic sin principle that results in sinful acts. We must not confuse this sin or flesh principle with the ego or self—the total person. The flesh refers to our ever-present propensity to rebellion and sin. It is *not* our total self and should not form the basis of our self-esteem.

Perhaps an illustration will show the difference between the ego, or self, and the flesh. If you place a few drops of ink in a glass of water, the ink will discolor and ruin the water. But is the ink the same as the water? Not really. The ink exists within the water, discoloring and polluting it, but it is not identical with the water. In order to overcome the negative effects of the ink, we don't throw out the water. That defeats our purpose. Instead we simply neutralize the ink.

So, too, our flesh, our rebellious sin principle, has discolored our entire self. Consequently, we need to overcome its all-pervading presence. But the answer is not to discard the self. Instead, we must overcome the influence of the flesh. This process is much like dealing with a diseased tree. We can look at a beautiful tree that is diseased and say, "That's a bad tree. We'd better chop it down." In doing that, we are identifying the tree on the basis of the disease. We are saying that the most basic thing about the tree is the disease. Or we can say, "That's a good tree with a disease. Let's treat the disease." In this case, we are identifying the tree by referring to its basic nature. We value the tree, but recognize that it has a problem.

In the same way, we need to base our identity on our total person and not on our tendency to sin. If we base our identity on our sinfulness, we set ourselves up to be knocked down by a lack of self-acceptance. If, however, we base our identity on our total person as created by God, we can begin laying a foundation for an attitude of self-acceptance.

Paul speaks of the difference between our ego, or self, and our sinfulness. "As it is, it is no longer I myself who do it, but it is sin living in me. I know that nothing good lives in *me*, that is, in my *sinful nature* [italics added]. For I have the desire to do what is good, but I cannot carry it out" (Rom. 7:17-18). Paul is saying that it is not his "I" (ego—his total self) doing the evil, but sin that dwells in him.

If we stopped reading after the first part of verse eighteen, we would have the impression that there is nothing worthwhile in Paul. But the last part of verse eighteen makes it clear that he is referring specifically to his sinful tendency and not to his total person. In verses 21-23, Paul explains that his rebellious tendencies are not the same as his self. He delights in the law of God with his inner man, his deepest nature that desires to do good and follow God. But another law, the law of sin, continues to fight against his deep desires toward God.

Paul had made a similar distinction earlier. "In the same way,

count yourselves dead to sin but alive to God in Christ Jesus"
(Rom. 6:11). Some people have manipulated this verse to say that
we should crucify ourselves or our ego. This viewpoint is false. To
begin with, Paul says that as Christians we have *already* died with
Christ (Rom. 6:6). Crucifixion is not something *we* do; it is something that *Christ* has already done. Neither does Paul say that our
total personality or self is to be considered dead. Rather, he says
that we are to consider ourselves dead to sin but alive to God. Our
self is to be very much alive, but it should be alive and responsive
to God.

Notes

1. It is the nominative case of the first person pronoun.
2. For a thorough treatment of New Testament uses of *ego*, see *Theological Dictionary of the New Testament*, ed. Gerhard Kittel, trans. Geoffrey Bromiley, vol. 2 (Grand Rapids: Eerdmans, 1964).
3. W. B. Vine, *Expository Dictionary of New Testament Words* (Old Tappan, N. J.: Fleming H. Revell, 1946), p. 341.
4. Ibid., p. 202.
5. Ibid., pp. 107-8.

Humility: What It is and Isn't

Humility: What It is and Isn't

In a Christian organization where I worked there was a woman who thought she was extremely humble. She was a secretary, and she seemed obsessed with being both spiritual and humble. She walked around with a very sad and depressed look. At devotions, she often shared her gratitude to God for accepting someone as terrible as she. One day she said to me, "Bruce, aren't you glad that we are nothing and God is so good?" When I hesitated to agree, she added, "I just wish more people realized that they really are nothing. Then God could really be exalted."

Humility Is Not Inferiority

Like that woman, many people confuse humility with inferiority. To these people, humility is considering themselves less valuable or capable than others. They reason, *If we esteem ourselves more lowly than others, then we are being humble and following God's command.* Under the guise of spiritual commitment, they engage in perpetual self-debasement to try to find true victory in the Christian life. They believe that if they can only rid themselves of all ability and desire, God will enter their life and take over. Entire Christian movements have been based on this assumption.

People who hold to this concept of humility often quote Philippians 2:3 to support their view. "Do nothing from selfishness or empty conceit, but with humility of mind let each of you regard one another as more important than himself (NASB)." At first glance, this passage seems to suggest that Christians should feel inferior. But as is frequently the case, a careful reading of the context sheds a very different light. Let's read the passage in its entirety:

> Make my joy complete by being of the same mind, maintaining the same love, united in spirit, intent on one purpose. Do nothing from selfishness or empty conceit, but with humility of mind let each of you regard one another as more important than himself; do not *merely* look out for your own personal interests, but also for the interests of others. Have this attitude in yourselves which was also in Christ Jesus, who, although He existed in the form of God, did not regard equality with God a thing to be grasped, but emptied Himself, taking the form of a bond-servant, *and* being made in the likeness of men. And being found in appearance as a man, He humbled Himself by becoming obedient to the point of death, even death on a cross. Therefore also God highly exalted Him, and bestowed on Him the name which is above every name. (Phil. 2:2-9 NASB).

Through these writings, Paul challenged the church to be unified and warned the Philippians about the dangers of sinful pride. He speaks of: (1) being of the same mind; (2) maintaining the same love; (3) having a unity of spirit; and (4) being intent on one purpose. He then mentions the attitudes that can ruin this unity—specifically, selfishness and conceit. Within this context, Paul writes, "With humility of mind let each of you regard one another as more important than himself." Then he goes on to explain what he means by humility of mind and regarding one another as more important than himself. He states that Christ is our example and that we should have the attitude that was in Christ.

Paul then describes Christ's humility in verses five and following. These verses give four ingredients of Christ's humility.

- He had a high position with God.
- He took a position low in service but high in worth.
- He was obedient even to death.
- He was exalted after His death.

According to Paul, Christ is our example of humility. Notice the absence of any suggestion of inferiority or any self-degrading statements. Christ certainly did not see Himself as inferior or worthless in the sight of other men. He never said, "I am so wretched and low that I might as well be the one to volunteer to go to the cross." He saw Himself as an image-bearer. He knew His value, His worth, and His identity.

Since Christ had a secure identity, He didn't have to flaunt his strengths. He was free to put aside His own interests for the benefit of others. Humility hinges on this important point. Even though Christ was God, He willingly humbled Himself, became a servant, and obeyed His Father in all aspects of His earthly life. Our humility should be the same. In fact, there are some striking parallels. Notice that we, like Christ:

- Have a high position as God's children and image-bearers.
- Can take a position low in service but high in worth.
- Can be obedient to God until death.
- Will be exalted as we reign with Christ forever.

When Paul told us to esteem ourselves below others, he was neither implying that we are worthless or challenging us to feel inferior. Instead, he was saying that as people with a secure identity, we are to focus on the needs of others and how we can minister to them.

Some of us shy away from likening ourselves to Christ. We feel a little anxious to even entertain the thought. *After all,* we reason, *He is God. How dare we compare ourselves with Him?* Yet Christ is the model that Paul held out to us. The "attitude" Paul refers to in verse five is an attitude of love, one accord, the esteem of others, and service. If we are going to maintain a proper attitude toward ourselves, we must understand that biblical humility starts with Christ's example. Humility is not inferiority.

Humility Is Not the Underestimation of Our Abilities

Underestimating our abilities is closely related to the "humility as inferiority" concept. Some people take 2 Corinthians 12:9, "my power is made perfect in weakness," to mean that the more inadequate a person is, the more God will be glorified. In fact, it leads to a degradation of God's creation.

While it is true that apart from a vital union with Christ our lives will bear little or no spiritual fruit, humility does not mean the denial of our natural God-given abilities. Paul's statement must be understood in context. He was speaking about his problem with pride. In verse seven of the same chapter, Paul comments about his vision from God and the possibility of using that gift to exalt himself over others. "To keep me from becoming conceited . . . there was given me a thorn in my flesh."

Paul does not say that he lacked abilities. He does not say that he had a low IQ, couldn't speak before a crowd, or had little to contribute to life. On the contrary, Paul was one of the brightest, most educated, and articulate men of his day. Describing himself, Paul writes, "I ought to have been commended by you, for I am not in the least inferior to the 'super-apostles,' even though I am nothing" (2 Cor. 12:11). God wanted Paul to have a balanced image of himself, to know his own abilities. But He did not want Paul to forget that he, too, needed God's continual presence to carry out his ministry.

John 3:22-30 is another passage that is often taken out of context to support self-belittling attitudes. John the Baptist, referring to Christ, says, "He must become greater; I must become less important" (3:30). John is not saying that he is worthless and knows that his efforts will come to nothing. The context makes it clear that he is responding to some people who were trying to stir up conflict between him and Christ by saying, "Rabbi, that man who was with you on the other side of the Jordan—the one about whom you testified—well, he is baptizing, and everyone is going to him" (3:26).

John responded quickly to this challenge. "A man can receive only what is given him from heaven. You yourselves can testify that I said, 'I am not the Christ but am sent ahead of him'"

(3:27-28). He adds: "The one who comes from above is above all; the one who is from the earth belongs to the earth . . ." (3:31). John was not putting on inferiority; he wanted Christ to be recognized as God and he sought to live out his role as the forerunner who would make Christ, not himself, well-known.

Humility Is Not Self-hatred

I frequently encounter people suffering from depression. Generally these people are friendly, cooperative, and kind; and their friends cannot understand the depression that haunts them.

Underneath their friendly and cooperative image, however, lie strong feelings of bitterness and resentment. Rather than directing these feelings toward others, however, these people direct their anger inward. Constantly "down" on themselves, they never give themselves credit for accomplishments. Instead, they repeatedly berate and criticize themselves.

If they are Christians, they are usually exceedingly sensitive to sin. They experience guilt and confess their sins at the slightest tinge of conscience. They make repeated trips to the altar to make sure of their spiritual well-being. When they read the Bible, verses on sin and judgment leap out at them and they use them to punish themselves with their emotions. They are often among the most committed church members, genuinely seeking God's will for their lives. Unfortunately, however, their entire Christian experience is distorted by their self-hatred. This self-inflicted punishment is certainly not humility; it is actually a form of masochism. Why should anyone hate what God created, loves, and redeemed with His Son's death?

Humility Is Not Passivity

I grew up in a farming community in Arizona during the 1940s and early '50s. Our little community had one five-room schoolhouse, one store (which doubled as the post office), one service station (long since closed), and one small Baptist church. Nearly everyone attended this church—at least on special occasions such as Christmas, Easter, weddings, and funerals. It played an important role in the spiritual and social life of our community.

Yet, as I recall, most of the male leaders in the church were rather passive. The ministers were not strong, aggressive, or highly respected. Although the dedicated lay leaders were respected for their service in the church, they certainly were not the most successful farmers and ranchers of the area. In fact, while growing up, I had the distinct impression that Christianity and successful farming did not mix. Unfortunately, many people still equate Christianity with passivity and weakness.

During a recent seminar, I asked the two hundred participants to think of the most humble person they knew. I then asked them to list the five words that best described that person. This gave us 1,000 statements about "humble" people. The results were interesting. Two traits stood out above all others. The first was a warm loving attitude. The second was a quiet, or unassuming, manner. Humble people, according to the survey, were *loving* and *quiet*. Love is certainly a key ingredient in humility. But since when is quietness necessary for humility? These people, like many of us, had some serious misunderstandings about humility.

Among the phrases used to describe a humble person, there were several glaring omissions. Not once, for example, did anyone ascribe the characteristics of aggressiveness, boldness, intelligence, enthusiasm, or ambition to a humble person. Apparently if we are intelligent and aggressive, we can't be humble!

Close your eyes for a moment and picture an extremely humble person. Do you see a weak, quiet, or passive person? Many of us do. But these characteristics are not outgrowths of genuine humility, for humility is really based on strength.

Once again, Christ is our example. When it was appropriate, He showed His strength and boldness. Righteously angry, He entered the temple, drove out all who were buying and selling, and overturned the tables of the moneychangers and the benches of those selling doves (Matt. 21:12). Then he said, "It is written, 'My house will be called a house of prayer,' but you are making it a 'den of robbers'" (Matt. 21:13).

Christ also showed His strength by being willing to suffer great pain and insult on the cross at the hands of others. People challenged Him, "Come down from the cross, if you are the Son of

God!" (Matt. 27:40). He allowed them to mock Him and spit in His face—a most severe form of public humiliation. But He didn't do it out of weakness, as if He was too fearful or cowardly to fight back. He could have had the entire group destroyed with one cry, but He hung on the cross because of His love for us.

No, humility is not passivity. The truly humble person is confident of both his strength and his rights. With his strength, he can choose to take a position of service or suffering, if that is called for. Because of his inner strength, he can also rise up and aggressively combat evil when circumstances call for action.

We have seen what humility is not. It is not inferiority, underestimation of our abilities, self-hatred, or passivity. But if humility is none of these, then what is it?

Humility Is Recognizing Our Need of God

The Old Testament records many miracles that God performed during Israel's beginning years. He sent plagues of insects, frogs, and boils to the Egyptians. He parted the waters of the Red Sea, allowing the Israelites to escape the fierce Egyptian army. And He repeatedly provided food and water for His people. In spite of all these miracles, God believed it necessary to give Israel still another reminder of their need to rely on Him.

> And you shall remember all the way which the Lord your God has led you in the wilderness these forty years, that He might humble you, testing you, to know what was in your heart, whether you would keep his commandments or not. And he humbled you and let you be hungry, and fed you with manna which you did not know . . . that He might make you understand that man does not live by bread alone, but man lives by everything that proceeds out of the mouth of the Lord. Your clothing did not wear out on you, nor did your foot swell these forty years. . . . Therefore, you shall keep the commandments of the Lord your God, to walk in His ways and to fear Him. For the Lord your God is bringing you into a good land, a land of brooks of water, of fountains and springs, flowing forth in valleys and hills; a land of wheat and barley, of vines and fig trees and pomegranates. . . . Beware lest you forget the Lord your God by not keeping His commandments and His ordinances and His statutes

> which I am commanding you today; lest, when you have
> eaten and are satisfied, and have built good houses and lived
> *in them,* and when your herds and your flocks multiply, and
> your silver and gold multiply, and all that you have multi-
> plies, then your heart becomes proud, and you forget the
> LORD your God who brought you out from the land of Egypt,
> out of the house of slavery (Deut. 8:2-4, 6-8, 11-14).

Through Moses, God once again reminded the Israelites of the purpose of their wilderness wandering. It was designed to teach them to depend on Him—to learn personal and national humil-ity. Similarly, God wants us to recognize our need of Him. He wants us to acknowledge that He created us, that He built into us the elements of His image, and that we must rely on Him to provide each of us a full and meaningful life (Matt. 6:33). This is the framework for biblical humility.

Recognizing our place in God's creation is the essence of humil-ity. God is the Creator, we are the created. God is the central character; we are the supporting cast. Although we can ac-complish many things, we cannot function at our best without a recognition of our need of Him.

Humility Is Realistically Evaluating Our Capacities

Once we recognize that we are valuable as created children of God, we can begin to realistically evaluate our strengths and limitations. Every person who has ever lived has had some talent, some gift, some contribution that he could make to life. Paul writes that we each have different gifts and should "exercise them accordingly" (Rom. 12:6 NASB). But he also writes earlier in that chapter that we should not think so highly of ourselves that we vaunt ourselves above others in the body (Rom. 12:3). The body of Christ requires many members with different gifts operating together in love (1 Cor. 12). A humble person must take stock of his gifts in order to use them as a member of a team and should not elevate himself above others or lower himself to the dregs.

Humility Is Being Willing to Serve

Shortly before His crucifixion, Christ and the disciples were together in the upper room. During the meal, a dispute arose among the disciples as to who was the greatest. To settle the squabble, Jesus said, "The kings of the Gentiles lord it over them; and those who exercise authority over them are given the title Benefactor. But you are not to be like that. Instead, the greatest among you should be like the youngest, and the one who rules like the one who serves" (Luke 22:25-26).

Like many of us, the disciples had a problem about who was the greatest. But Jesus shook their human standards when He said that Christianity has a different goal. While the secular world has a hierarchy of strength, power, and wealth, God's hierarchy includes loving service to others. Christ was the greatest, but He served. He washed the disciples' feet and suffered utmost humiliation for others. Through these and other acts, He demonstrated another aspect of humility: the willingness to serve. This service, however, comes from inner strength, rather than weakness. Some people become servants because they think they can't do anything else. They serve out of weakness instead of strength. But this is not humility.

Jesus didn't go passively to the cross because He was the least desirable of all Christians. He didn't say, "Someone has to die and I guess I'm the least important of everyone so I'll volunteer." Instead, conscious of His own identity before God, He *confidently* became a servant—even to the point of death. Likewise, when we reach out to others from an attitude of inner strength, we are experiencing a key ingredient of humility.

Biblical humility can be summarized as follows:

Humility	
Is Not	**Is**
1. Inferiority	1. A balanced self-esteem
2. Underestimation of our abilities	2. Realistically evaluating our abilities
3. Self-hatred	3. Recognizing our need of God
4. Passivity	4. Being willing to serve the needs of others

The Birth of Self-acceptance

The Birth of Self-acceptance

A newborn infant lying in his crib isn't equipped with instant self-esteem. He doesn't smile, open his eyes, and good-naturedly say, "Good morning world. Here I am. I like myself and I like you. Let's get this show on the road." In fact, he doesn't even know he exists. He does experience heat and cold, hunger and thirst, pain and pleasure, loud and soft noises, and other basic physical sensations, but at this point in his development he has no concept of himself as a distinct person. He literally does not know that his mother is another distinct individual. He has neither a physical nor an emotional self-image. He is simply a bundle of possibilities waiting for his innate potential and the influence of his environment to mold him into an independent person. And he is about to begin a journey that will shape his entire attitude toward himself. The way he makes this journey, and the help he gets along the way, will determine the essential make-up of his self-concept.

The First Twelve Months

During his first year of life, an infant's central nervous system develops rapidly and a variety of body processes mature. After having been in total union with his mother during pregnancy, the infant gradually realizes that he is an individual person. At first, this is a very vague perception. He begins to realize that there are some things "out there" (chairs, bottles, and toys) and some things "right here" (hands, feet, and fingers). Some things, like hands and feet, go with him everywhere. Other things, like chairs and bottles, don't always tag along.

Although he can't consciously think the words, he slowly learns that certain things "right here" are always with him, while the things "out there" are not. And when he puts the "right here" things in his mouth, it is a feeling different than the "out there" things. In fact, he soon derives pleasure from sucking on his hands or even his feet! These experiences gradually help the infant begin to discriminate between himself and his environment. He begins to find out what things make up his person and what things do not. This development is the beginning of his first self-image, the physical self-image. This is the forerunner of later, more specific, attitudes toward himself and is the soil from which his adult self-concept will grow.

Since the infant's first self-awareness is largely physical, physical experiences play a major role in the attitudes he develops about himself. If he is held, fed, and physically cared for, his first experiences will be positive. If his mother, or mother substitute, provides him with a comfortable and tension-free environment, he will feel relatively calm, peaceful, and self-satisfied. His first concept of himself and life will be good.

If, however, his first few months are not positive, the infant's first self-concept may be very different. The early months of life for some children are punctuated by repeated periods of physical cold, hunger, or thirst. Their mothers are either absent or extremely tense and high-strung. This causes more tension, anxiety, and frustration than the infant can handle and lays a shaky foundation for their later emotional adjustment. This introduces a fascinating story from medical history.

> Several decades ago, one of the most baffling problems of child health was a disease known as marasmus. The name

comes from a Greek word which meant "wasting away." Marasmus affected particularly children in the first year of life, and at that time it was responsible for more than half the deaths of babies in that age group. . . .

For some unknown reason otherwise healthy babies just wasted away, became very weak emotionally and physically, and sometimes died. To combat this tragic evil a special study of infant care was undertaken by both medical and social agencies, and the astonishing discovery was made that babies in the best homes and hospitals, given the most careful physical attention, sometimes drifted into this condition of slow dying, while infants in the poorest homes, with a loving mother, often overcame the handicaps of poverty and unhygienic surroundings and became bouncing babies. It was found that the element lacking in the sterilized lives of the babies of the former class, and generously supplied to those that flourished in spite of hit or miss environmental conditions, was mother love. A new system of carefully selecting foster mothers was developed, and, whenever an infant had no suitable person to care for him, he was sent to a foster home rather than to an institution. Young infants are now kept in hospitals for as short a time as possible. As a result, marasmus has become a rare disease.[1]

The scientifically "startling" discovery that the lack of physical mothering in an infant's early months can lead to serious illness and death is just one evidence of the tremendous impact the first few months of life have on an infant. Even though none of us can recall anything specific that happened during this early period, our initial environment and early experiences are the foundation for our later emotional and physical adjustment. They go a long way in either providing a basic sense of security, trust, and self-acceptance, or in making it difficult for us to develop these constructive feelings.

Broadening Horizons

Toward the end of his first year, the infant begins to move around and explore his environment. He takes his first hesitating steps and learns his first simple words. Soon he is into everything in sight. Every dish, vase, lamp, and knickknack is a potential "find." For example, one day during his exploration, he picks up a heavy object and drops it. If it is a toy, he has nothing to worry about; he merely picks it up again. But if he has dropped a family heirloom or a breakable dish, he quickly finds himself in trouble. His mother or some ever-present adult shouts, "Watch out!" or "Be careful" or "No, no!" Immediately the child becomes anxious about himself and his activities. *I'd better watch out,* he thinks, *I've done something wrong and I'm bad.*

To better understand the toddler's perspective, imagine being placed on a distant planet where you confront an unknown civilization, a foreign language, and a world of strange objects. To top it all off, you are only one year old, so you can hardly talk and you don't know how to get along without your mother. Puzzled and bewildered, eventually you toddle over to an intriguing object, touch it, smile, and pick it up. Immediately a large spaceman comes by, grabs the object, and shouts, "No!" Frightened, you step back and busy yourself with something else. But each time you reach out to explore your world, you are rebuffed. After a series of these encounters, you begin to feel small, insignificant, and overwhelmed. You do not feel good about this world or your position in it.

This is the dilemma the toddler faces. Can he reach out and explore his environment comfortably, or must he hesitate each time he tries to learn more about his world? He is off to a good start if he is helped to enjoy his environment and himself. But if every attempt to reach out is met by anxiety or rebuke, he will have trouble feeling good about himself and his efforts.

Toward the end of his first year or so of life, the toddler begins to develop a clearer mental image of himself. His central nervous system has developed to the point that he knows himself from others and he is beginning to get a clearer picture of himself. But where does he turn to find this picture? He hasn't matured enough to make his own evaluations. He cannot look in a mirror and think, *I look fine today. Maybe I'm ready to go out and face the world.* His only mirror is the comments and evaluations he receives from others. So the next ingredient of the young child's self-esteem is the input he receives from the persons who are always nearby, his parents.

Parental Attitudes

Parents' feelings about their children fluctuate, and this is true for every parent. Sometimes parents are positive, sensitive, and loving. They help to instill a sense of worth, confidence, and esteem in their growing child. Sometimes, however, they attack the child's developing sense of self-worth and make him feel inadequate and inferior.

The interactions of a normal day give parents dozens of opportunities to shape their child's self-esteem. Mealtimes are a good example. In many families, this is the most difficult time of the day. Imagine that a child is reaching for some food and accidentally knocks over his glass of milk. The parent might shout, "Be careful!" or "Watch what you're doing!" or "What's the matter with you?" Immediately the child tenses up. He didn't try to spill his milk. Yet, because his attempt to reach his milk was unsuccessful, he is shamed and scolded for his efforts.

Let's see how the situation could have been handled. What if the mother or father simply said, "Oh, oh, there goes the milk" while reaching for a cloth to clean up the milk? This response would let the child know that he needs to be careful, but it would also preserve his self-esteem. He wouldn't feel clumsy, awkward, or stupid, and since he isn't made to feel more anxious, he is less likely to spill the milk again. What could have been a negative experience has turned into a learning situation; the child has learned that it is not good to spill milk and his self-esteem remains intact.

Several years ago, I had an experience that brought this home to me. My eight-year-old son, Dickie, and I drove downtown to get a pizza. We placed our order and did some window-shopping in nearby stores while we waited. After fifteen minutes or so, we picked up our pizza and headed toward the car. After Dickie opened the passenger door and climbed in, he said, "I'll take it!"

I set the pizza in his hands, but before I let go, I asked, "Are you sure you've got it?"

"Sure," he replied, a confident expression on his face.

You can guess what happened! Dickie dropped the pizza and most of it went upside down on the dusty floor of my Maverick.

My first impulse was to say, "What's the matter with you? I just
asked you if you had it! Why don't you be more careful?" But I
quickly caught myself when I realized the impact that such a
statement could have on his self-esteem. Instead, I looked at him
and said, "Oh, I guess we've got pizza upside-down cake!" Then
we both laughed and began to clean up the mess. When we
returned home, I asked Dickie to finish cleaning up the car so that
I wouldn't have to smell pizza on the way to work the next
morning. Afterward, we went into the house and ate what was left
of the pizza.

A few hours later, as I was putting Dickie to bed, he leaned up
on one elbow and said, "Dad, what would another dad have
done?"

Puzzled, I said, "What do you mean, Dickie?"

"About the pizza," he replied. "What would he have done if his
boy had dropped the pizza?"

"I don't know, son. What do you think?"

"I think he'd be mad!"

In some ways, this incident was minor, but it's just the sort of
interaction that molds self-esteem.

Parental Language and Self-esteem

The pizza incident leads us to another factor in self-esteem—
the labels we receive from our parents and others. Most parents
have a few favorite terms they use to motivate their children or to
express frustration. If a child sleeps too long, he is "lazy." If he
makes a mistake, he is "stupid." When he is uncooperative, he is
"stubborn." When he isn't mannerly, he is "gross." And when his
room is unkempt, he is "sloppy."

During a recent seminar for parents, I asked the participants to
write down the labels that had been applied to them during their
childhood. In addition to the ones already mentioned, the adults
listed "tank," "motor mouth," "leather gut," "beanpole," "pea
brain," "Simple Sally," "fat cow's tail," "grasshopper brain," and
"elephant ears." One lady even burst into tears as she recalled the
label "devil daughter." It was now forty years later, but she still
could not throw off the shackles of that distressing label.

Whenever a child is labeled, an image is written on his mind. Repeated labels influence a child who is shaping an image of himself. Accusations such as "clumsy" or "stupid" become important elements of the child's growing attitude toward himself. Absorbed and stored in his mind, these labels act as a barrier to his development of self-esteem.

Frequently these labels become so deeply embedded in our personality that they continue to exist even when there is no objective basis for them. A girl who is teased about her looks, for example, may never learn to like her appearance even after she has become a beautiful woman. A man labeled "stupid" as a child may still feel foolish even though he has a string of college degrees and has proven himself in business. The curse of childhood labeling and ridicule was clearly expressed to me by an attractive woman who said, "I don't care how beautiful people think I am. To me, I'm still an ugly girl from the wrong side of the tracks." Childhood ridicule overruled the reassurances of her friends because a contradictory image had been etched in her mind.

However, each time parents communicate respect, love, and trust to their child, they lay another building block in the foundation of that child's self-esteem. Praise, genuine acceptance, patience, and affirmation go a long way in helping a young child to cultivate a good attitude toward himself. Such responses from parents and other people help to form the roots of the child's self-acceptance.

Since no parent is perfect, we all enter adulthood with mixed feelings about our appearance, intelligence, and worth. If our parents were largely successful in communicating confidence and respect, we will tend to have a positive self-concept. But if they frequently attacked our self-esteem through criticism, ridicule, or anger, we will have real difficulty learning to like ourselves.

Notes

1. Margaret Ribble, *The Rights of Infants* (New York: Columbia University Press, 1965), pp. 4-5.

**Our
Ideal Self**

7
Our
Ideal Self

During the first decade or so of life, each of us encounters a variety of goals, ideals, and expectations. Our parents, for example, establish expectations. They expect us to be smart, pretty, athletic, talented, or nice. As young children, we are taught to say "Please," to stop fighting with our brothers and sisters, to pick up our room, and a thousand other things.

One couple I know demands that their children be perfectly polite. Every time the family goes out in public, they anxiously remind their children to mind their manners. The children must use "Yes sir," "Please," and "Thank you." The parents also remind the children when to smile and they never allow a "childish" word. In short, they demand perfection from their children, who are four and eight years old.

I have another acquaintance who is obsessed with his son's athletic prowess. He signs the boy up for every team sport, park program, and contest imaginable. He practices sports with his son after work and on the weekends, criticizing every flaw in his son's performance.

Obviously there is nothing wrong with manners or athletics. But these parents are exerting too much pressure on their children. They are holding out unrealistic and perfectionistic standards that will come back and haunt the child in later life. The polite child may learn his manners well, but he will probably lose his spontaneity and freedom in the process. The athletic child may become an excellent performer, but he will probably live under constant pressure to compete and excel. It is likely to drive him to ulcers.

Parents aren't the only source of unrealistic expectations. Television and radio project a variety of distorted images and ideals to the growing child. The successful person on television is attractive, intelligent, athletic, personable, and suave. Commercials tell us that soap will change our complexion, a six-week course will dramatically improve our memory, and toothpaste will give us sex appeal!

Consciously and unconsciously, these media goals and expectations merge with the ideals of our parents, peers, and teachers, and are absorbed into our personality. They come together to form a picture, a mental image, of what we think we want or ought to be.

Once these thoughts crystallize, this set of goals or expectations becomes our *ideal self*. It is the self we believe will make us happy if we can only reach it. It becomes the standard by which we judge ourselves and our performance. If we meet our ideal standards, we tend to like ourselves and experience self-esteem. But when we fall short of our ideals, we are left with feelings of discouragement or dissatisfaction. This ideal self, which is formed for the most part in the first decade or so of life, becomes a permanent fixture in our psychic lives. Years later, often without any awareness of it, we continue to judge ourselves by the standards we absorbed as children and young adults.

Your Punitive Self

At the same time our ideal self is forming, another equally important process is going on—the development of what I call our *punitive self*. Just as we take in our parents' ideals, we also internalize their methods of discipline as well as their attitudes about discipline. If parents repeatedly say, "Shame on you!" or "What's wrong with you?" or "That's stupid!" to a young child, he soon learns to think similar thoughts about himself when he falls short of his own or others' expectations. Just as his parents attack his self-esteem when he doesn't live up to their standards, he also learns to berate himself for falling short. This is a major cause of our inability to like ourselves. In many cases, such a person becomes his own worst enemy.

To understand how this process occurs, let's take a look at the negative messages parents can transmit. They can: (1) punish the child, physically or otherwise; (2) shame or berate the child by saying, "How awful!" or "Shame on you!"; (3) use anger to subtly reject the child; or (4) criticize the child directly or by comparing him with others. These four parental options are primary sources of our inability to love ourselves later in life.

Punishment

Let's look at punishment. A young child is told, "Since you did that, you must be punished." So when the child falls short of a parental standard, he soon learns to expect punishment. Repeated punishment deeply ingrains his thoughts. *When I fall short*, he muses, *I deserve to be punished.* While this thought is entirely natural, it is also the source of innumerable neurotic guilt feelings. Even as adults, we continue to operate on this balanced scale concept. When we fall short of our own or others' expectations, we begin to expect punishment or, in the absence of external punishment, to inflict pain on ourselves. A client of mine, for example, cut herself with a razor blade as a self-inflicted punishment. Torn with deep guilt feelings over her sexual behavior, she thought that this torture might atone for her misdeeds. Most of us, of course, don't inflict physical punishment on ourselves. Instead, we substitute mental pain or the expectation of punishment. We attack ourselves verbally with statements like, "How stupid of me" or "I failed" or "Now I am going to get caught and really get it!"

Self-depreciation

Another way parents frequently respond to misbehavior is to shame the child or give him a sense of self-depreciation. At one time or another, most parents have exclaimed, "Shame on you! You know better than that." Some parents go even further and say, "Look how you let us down. After all we've done for you, you have to hurt us this way!" Such comments, and the unspoken attitudes behind them, seriously undercut a young child's self-esteem and program him for a lack of self-acceptance.

Rejection

A third parental response to misbehavior is the veiled threat of rejection. We have all been on the receiving end of a loved one's anger. Parents, siblings, peers, or admired teachers have reacted to our misconduct with anger and frustration instead of loving concern. Their spankings or harsh words or angry looks communicated rejection. Under extreme duress, our parents may have even yelled, "I hate you!" or "Get out of my sight!"

One woman told me that she had great difficulty controlling her newly adopted daughter. "You can't imagine how I tried to get through to her," she said, "and nothing seemed to work. But now," she added proudly, "I've discovered a way that works. I tell her, 'God doesn't love you when you're naughty.'"

Sensing the deep rejection that her child must be feeling, I asked her, "Does God love you when you are naughty?"

She paused, somewhat taken aback, and then replied, "Oh, I get the point."

Most parents don't go to this extreme, but every parent is human and every growing child has experiences that communicate the message, "People love you less when you are naughty." Even the best of parents occasionally lose their temper and turn against their children.

Criticism

Criticism is another frequent parental response to a child's failure. Most parents naturally want their children to do better, and they believe that criticism is a good method for stimulating improvement. Usually, however, the opposite is true. I often tell parents that ninety-nine compliments barely make up for one criticism. Think back on your own life. Don't you remember criticism for a much longer time than praise? There is something about criticism that tears at our confidence and self-esteem. Although we like to believe that the criticism *we* give is just or contructive, this is usually not the case. People grow best through encouragement, support, and a positive example. Criticism damages a child's confidence and undermines his self-acceptance.

Our Loving Corrective Self

Fortunately the negative messages from our punitive self are only one side of the coin. Parents also have several options that serve to support and encourage their children. They can: (1) ignore the failure and let the child profit from the consequences of his action; (2) lovingly correct the child and help him to become more mature and self-confident; (3) set a better example; or (4) encourage the child.

For most of us, our parents also gave us "positive vibrations." Sometimes they loved us unconditionally and let us know it. When we failed and fell short of their expectations, they lovingly understood our anxiety and frustration. They lovingly corrected us and taught us more effective ways of coping with life. They let us know that we weren't expected to be perfect. And sometimes, instead of punishing, shaming, rejecting, or criticizing, they ignored our failures and showed us a better way through their words and example. To the degree our parents used these and other constructive forms of discipline, we internalized a positive set of corrective attitudes. I call this our *loving corrective self* and the attitudes and emotions that come from it are constructive forms of regret or godly sorrow (2 Cor. 7:9-10).

In contrast to the rejecting attitudes of the punitive self, our loving corrective self dispenses encouragement and support. It patiently stimulates our continued growth, following a model God laid out in Scripture. When the apostle John wrote to the church about sin, he stated, "My dear children, I write this to you so that you will not sin. But if anybody does sin, we have one who speaks to the Father in our defense—Jesus Christ, the Righteous One (1 John 2:1). Here we have a beautiful example of a positive parental attitude. God patiently motivates us and lovingly holds out His forgiveness during times when we fail. He doesn't respond to us angrily or with frustration.

Summary

We all enter adulthood with a set of goals or expectations—our ideal self. When we fall short of our ideals, our conscience triggers an awareness of our failure and sets in motion whatever corrective attitudes exist in our personality. If most of our parents' corrective attitudes were critical, harsh, or punitive, our punitive self responds to our adult failures with a similar attitude—self-rejection. If, on the other hand, our parents lovingly corrected us and refrained from shaming and criticizing us, we learned how to respond to our failures in a loving corrective way. Consequently, we are now able to admit our failures without putting ourselves under a pile of guilt, pressure, or condemnation. We can acknowledge our weaknesses and limitations while maintaining our self-esteem and self-acceptance.

If our parents were sensitive to our needs and feelings and didn't hold out unrealistic goals or punishment when we failed, we learned to accept ourselves even with our faults. If they relied on pressure, guilt, and shame, we absorbed these attitudes into our lives, making it difficult for us to love ourselves.

Three Enemies of Self-acceptance

8

Three Enemies of Self-acceptance

Now that we have looked at the development of self-esteem, we are ready to see why we have such difficulty maintaining self-acceptance. There are three major thought patterns or false assumptions that work against self-esteem. Let's take a look at the first assumption.

Acceptance Must Be Earned

Under the impact of our parents and others, we all develop the thought, *I must reach a certain standard of maturity, attitude, or achievement in order to be accepted.* Whether these are the standards of our parents, friends, teachers, pastors, or television heroes, we all begin to think that by reaching certain levels of accomplishment, we will be liked by others and consequently by ourselves. In other words, we learn to operate on the assumption that love is something earned by fulfilling expectations.

This assumption can severely inhibit the development of self-love. In fact, it is perhaps the most important cause of a lack of self-esteem. As long as we believe that we must *do* something in order to be loved, our sense of being loved is fragile. As long as we operate on this assumption, we approach life with the question, *How do others think I should act or react?* We learn to read our parents and others and to sense what they want from us. We learn how to please teachers, friends, and parents. And we learn to shape our lives by *others'* expectations. We do all this in the hope of finding a deep sense of security and love.

Unfortunately, it doesn't work. Just the reverse happens. In trying to mold our lives to earn the love of others, we actually short-circuit the process we need most. We develop an external view of who God intends us to be. We learn to squelch our spontaneity and freedom because we find that they don't always fit with others' wishes for us. And we try to develop some ability (be it athletics, music, aesthetics, or personality) to please our parents and others. In the process, our God-given gifts, capacities, and contributions are pushed into the background. We begin to develop a self that isn't our true self, but rather our image of what others think we are or should become. This false self-actualization causes us to lose touch with the creative, loving, spontaneous person God intends us to be.

One way to understand what happens here is to spend several hours watching one- or two-year-olds. Notice how alive, free, and happy they always seem to be? But then look at the same children ten to twenty years later. Chances are that much of their liveliness has long since vanished. Somewhere in the process of growing up, they lost touch with their spontaneous, happy, and enriching self. They lost it because, under the impact of parents and others, they developed the assumption, *I must meet other people's standards and expectations if I am going to be accepted or loved.* In other words, they traded a spontaneous sensitivity to their true self for an external conformity to the thoughts and expectations of others. Now, after many years, they have almost forgotten what it's like to relax, enjoy life, and allow their true feelings to surface.

Does this sound like you? It probably does, because all of us undergo part of this unfortunate process. Because we want the love of others so badly, we go to extremes to find it. The unfortunate thing is that in searching for others' love, we rob ourselves of what we have to give. We end up out of touch with the many creative, sensitive resources that God placed in us at the moment of our conception.

Failure Deserves Punishment

As we saw earlier, we take in our parents' corrective attitudes and actions just as we take in their goals, ideals, and expectations. To the degree our parents resorted to pressure, fear, shame, or guilt to motivate us, we developed a second false assumption. This is summed up in the thought, *When I fall short of my goals or expectations, I need to be pressured, shamed, frightened, or punished.*

Years of experience in being punished or corrected leave most of us with the deeply ingrained belief that whenever we fall short of our goals, we need to be pressured or in some way punished. By adulthood, our reaction has become entirely automatic. Even in our parents' absence, we verbally harass ourselves. Just like a parent who nags their child to "take out the trash," "clean your room," or "finish your supper," our internalized "parent" continues this silent pressure. It tells us to hurry up, to be more careful, to plan better, to work harder, or to achieve more. Rarely does it say, "Relax and enjoy life" or "You've done a good job" or "We all make mistakes" or "That's O.K. You did the best you could."

Our pressuring, punishing self, in other words, is stronger than our loving, corrective self. Because our parents didn't know how to lovingly accept us and gradually help us develop our capacities, we now resort to the same type of pressure that they exerted on us years earlier. We operate on the assumption learned from them that whenever we fall short, we should be punished or in some way pressured. In chapter twelve, we will examine the alternative to this type of pressure.

There is a third assumption that tears away at self-esteem. Unlike the first two, this assumption does not come from our parents or environment. Instead, it comes directly from our inner

life and exists regardless of the quality of our relationships with
our parents.

We Should Live Up To Our Own Wishes and Ideals

To understand this assumption, let's review our infancy. During our first few weeks and months of life, most of us live in a state
of comparative ease. Our mother drops whatever she is doing to
care for our wishes and our needs. When we are hungry, we are
fed. When we are thirsty, we are given a drink. When we are
cold, we are covered or held. Things revolve around our needs so
that in many ways we are like a tiny king. Our helplessness makes
everyone our servant; our wish is their command. For months
this continues. Time after time, people cater to our needs until
we develop the grand illusion that *we* are the center of the
universe.

This arrangement is both comfortable and necessary for the
infant, since he is completely dependent on other people for his
survival. Unfortunately, that state can't go on forever. At some
point, our parents decide that infancy—with all its attendant
pampering and permissiveness—is over, and we are now considered to be young children. From that moment on, they will no
longer cater to our every whim. This decision has tremendous
consequences for our emotional development.

Once our parents decide that we have matured enough that we
no longer always need to have our way, our illusion that we are at
the center of our environment is shattered. We quickly discover
that we can't always have our own way and that we too have
limitations and must endure frustration. After months of "king-
ship," we do not easily accept this rude awakening. We are in no
way ready to give up our position of power and control to become
aware of our weakness, inadequacy, or dependency. We do not
want to acknowledge our helplessness, to see our frailty, to give
up control of our environment, and to begin to live with limitations. We want to continue to feel strong, powerful, and in
control.

To understand the young child's perspective, imagine that you
are a small person in an adult world. Let's say that you are one or

two years old and weigh approximately thirty pounds. Your parents, five or six feet tall, weigh between one and two hundred pounds. In other words, they are about five times your size. By adult standards, your parents would be about twenty-five feet tall and weigh approximately seven hundred fifty pounds. Now imagine these giants towering over you. One of them cooks your meals and the other tells you when to eat. One of them tells you to pick up your toys and the other tells you that you can play. Wherever you go and whatever you do, these giants are always watching. Occasionally one of them loses his temper and scolds you in a loud, displeasing voice or whacks you with his hand. Although you sense that they love you, their tremendous size doesn't give you a great feeling of confidence and power. In fact, you probably feel extremely small and insignificant.

In your world of giants, there are many other people. Some of them, like you, are also called children, but even most of them are twice your size. And they, too, have many advantages over you. They can read and write, go to overnight parties at their friends' homes, stay up late, whip you in a fight, and get more privileges in almost every situation.

Coupled with your smallness over against your parents' and siblings' size and power, these things make you feel extremely weak and helpless. You have suddenly gone from having the world revolve around your needs to being acutely aware of your weaknesses, inadequacies, and inferiorities. You believe that your parents are extremely strong and smart. They can lift huge objects and answer any question. They can go anywhere they please, do anything they desire, and be exactly what they want. From your perspective, they are gods who rule the world and you are merely an inferior creature.

This displacement from center stage and its related godlike perception of parents drastically affects the development of every human being and leads to the third false assumption that undermines self-esteem. This assumption states, *Somehow, I can regain the comfort, security, and strength I felt when I was the center of my environment; I can master my world and become a "god" like my parents.*

Every person believes that once he becomes as big, as smart, and as powerful as his parents, he will have it made. We want to throw off all vestiges of our childish inferiority and master our environment. The two-year-old can hardly wait until he is three. The three-year-old can hardly wait until he is four. The junior high student can hardly wait for high school. The high school student can hardly wait for graduation or his first full-time job. And on it goes. Even as adults, we continue to strive toward our ideal view of the perfect adult. Such an achievement, we feel, is the only solution to our helpless state and its consequent anxiety. We each think, *When I am big, I will be in control. I will be smart, have money, and make my own decisions.* In short, we believe that when we become like our parents, we will be able to control our life and ward off all feelings of hopelessness and anxiety. Unfortunately, this effort is doomed to failure.

Regaining Power Through Manipulation

Even a child knows he isn't like his giant parents. So he looks for ways to regain either his position as the center of attention or the sense of power he once had. Some children try hard to become intelligent, strong, or good, and in these ways regain a sense of strength. Others turn to more devious or mischievous ways.

The typical two-year-old, for example, refuses to cooperate with most parental dictums. If the parent says, "Eat," the child says, "No!" If the parent says, "It's time for bed," the child says, "No!" No matter what the parent suggests, the child takes the opposite side. This is his way of gaining power and control.

Other children manipulate by throwing tantrums, becoming "ill," "forgetting" to do their chores, or always being late for dinner. All of these efforts, however, are designed to regain a sense of security, strength, or power. They are attempts to ward off feelings of being small, helpless, weak, and insignificant, and to show parents who's boss. They are the child's attempt to become like a god.

Carried into adulthood, some of these strategies become extremely difficult to recognize. The original struggle for power and control is lost under seemingly innocent reactions. Who would think that people who are repeatedly late, for example, are displaying an underlying need for power and control? Most of us know someone who is this way. Getting ready for work or school or church always seems to be a hassle. They are usually just a little late. So they get up a little earlier or they try to hurry. They scurry around the house under immense pressure, but still they don't make it. No matter how early they begin, something always comes about to make them late again. This is not merely chance. People who are perpetually late are usually saying, "Don't rush me. I'll get ready in my own time frame!" As children, these people usually had at least one parent who pressured or coerced them. Lateness became a good way to rebel or to get power over the pressuring parent.

Other children learn to give up in the face of their parents' demands. They become depressed or passive. Now, as adults, they are painfully aware of feelings of helplessness, inferiority, and depression. They rarely feel like trying to achieve and have withdrawn from any aggressive effort. They feel totally inadequate. But have you ever noticed the side effects of depression and withdrawal? When we become helpless, what do others do? Don't they often step up and encourage us, help us with our work, or somehow change their schedule to help us cope with our depression? Becoming helpless and weak like an infant does have some advantages. Even though it is painful and degrading, in an unconscious sort of way depression can be an attempt to return to the comforts of infancy and helplessness in the face of a world that seems too big to handle alone. In this way, even depression and feelings of inferiority may contain an element of controlling others and getting them to do our bidding.

So, from infancy on, we look for ways to get our way, to demonstrate our authority, or to prove our adequacy. We become stubborn, competitive, likeable, aggressive, quiet, argumentative, or whatever we believe we need to become, in an attempt to overcome our feelings of inferiority and weakness. Sometimes our attempts temporarily relieve our feelings of inadequacy. But no matter how well we perform or how frequently we win out over our parents in daily struggles, we still don't fully succeed in throwing off the shackles of inferiority. We can never be in full control or become the perfect giants we see our parents to be.

Regaining Power Through Fantasy

In the face of this failure, we develop still another way to regain our self-respect. We learn to fantasize and daydream about power and achievement. We develop a mental picture of ourselves performing unusual accomplishments or great feats. In our dreams, we become an athletic hero, a beauty queen, a famous teacher, or a politician. Through fantasy, we try to find the success and strength we wish we had in reality. We accomplish the prodigious feats of giants and temporarily master all our feelings of inferiority. We create a mental image of ourselves in which we are just the way we would like to be.

These fantasies aren't necessarily bad. They can add spice to life and be a source of motivation. But they can also lead to serious problems, since after prolonged periods of imagination we become increasingly dissatisfied with our actual achievements. Every time we feel we are inferior, inadequate, or a failure, we turn to daydreams for our satisfaction. Here we are the masters of our fate once again. Unscathed, we accomplish our every wish, but an unfortunate perspective is set up in the process. When we don't live up to the ideals of our dreams, we begin to be less than satisfied with ourselves. We judge ourselves by our fantasized ideals and consider ourselves failures if we don't reach the fantastic expectations of our dreams. Even though we consciously know that these ideals are unrealistic, we cling to them hoping that by some miracle they will come true.

At a recent seminar for pastors and their wives, I asked the participants to share their secret fantasies and ideals. One husky fellow immediately raised his hand. "I'd like to be a baseball hero." A rather stocky woman wanted to be a ballet dancer. Another wanted to be a concert pianist. Others wanted to be beauty queens, outstanding evangelists, renowned authors, and a variety of other ideal personages.

These goals—seemingly innocuous—can program us for failure and a lack of self-esteem, since we can never fulfill our childish expectations. Similar to the way our parents' ideals became absorbed into our lives, our own goals and wishes—no matter how fantastic—become ingrained in our minds and measure our performance. If our accomplishments measure up to our expectations, we reward ourselves with doses of self-esteem and self-acceptance. If our accomplishments don't satisfy us, however, we punish ourselves with varying amounts of self-criticism, guilt, and shame.

Every time we evaluate ourselves, we compare ourselves to unrealistic standards and expectations instead of to normal, human goals. Our measuring rod is the all-knowing and all-powerful twenty-five-foot giant or the unfettered hero of our dreams.

You can see the problem that this set of attitudes causes. Instead of growing up to become reasonably intelligent, strong, and autonomous adults (as God intended), we try to become *the* strongest, *the* smartest, *the* prettiest, or in some way, *the* best. Consciously or unconsciously, we try to become like our idealized parents because we thought they had everything under control. Like our parental values and expectations, these fantasized goals and expectations become part of our emotional and mental life—additional ingredients of our ideal self. Now every time we attempt to learn to love ourselves, these unrealistic goals surface and say, *You're not good enough, you don't measure up*, or You *don't deserve to love yourself because you aren't perfect!* No matter how well we do, we can never be satisfied with our achievements. Our goals of power and perfection have returned to haunt us.

Even after we become successful and achieve many of our goals, we may still feel dissatisfied and start looking for other areas in which to excel. Our grades are never quite high enough. Our homes are never quite nice enough. Our job is never quite good enough. And our children are never quite well-behaved enough. No matter how good we get, there is always something else we could or should be doing. We may have the height, weight, job, age, education—everything we need to finally be "big." On the outside, we meet every qualification and should be content. But inside, the feeling that we still lack something nags at us. No matter how many times we tell ourselves that we have arrived, our self-doubts linger. Our idealized self is too unrealistic and has become deeply embedded in our personality. The moment our achievements fail to reach our fantasized ideal expectations, we are immediately vulnerable to self-criticism and rejection We can't truly accept ourselves because we aren't living up to our own unrealistic expectations.

Regaining Power Through Playing God

The insatiable ambition to fulfill the glory of our dreams is closely tied in to another mental attitude that we all develop. This is the attitude that says, *I know best what will fulfill my happiness and my needs; I know best what will make me happy.* Beginning with childhood experiences—wanting another candy bar, wanting to go out and play, not wanting to do our chores—we all developed the thought, *If I were in control, everything would be O.K.!*

This idea carries over beautifully into adulthood. We think, *I know how intelligent I should be. I know how attractive I should be. I know how successful I should be.* We set ourselves up as the one who knows best what's good for us. In other words, we take on the role of God.

This setting ourselves up as a god is actually the essential ingredient of sin. Think back to Adam and Eve. They were the first people to become dissatisfied with their human limitations and decide that they knew best how they should be. They decided it was not enough to be the children God created them to be. Wanting to become something more, they decided to become like God. Just like a child who is not satisfied with his limitations, Adam and Eve decided that they would become like their twenty-five-foot giant Parent. To understand the parallel, let's take a look at this intriguing story.

When God placed Adam and Eve in the Garden, He established a certain order. As the Creator, He was at the center. Next came the angels, followed by man, then the animal and vegetable kingdoms. Man was purposely placed in a lofty position. Created in the image of God, man was set far above the animals. He was given great beauty, intellect, and power. But as part of creation, he was clearly ranked lower than God.

In his role on earth, man had a twofold obligation. He was to be the divinely appointed governor of earth, but had to remain obedient to God. Given authority over the earth, man was placed under the authority of God. He had great built-in capacities, but also certain limitations. Like God, he had intelligence. Unlike God, he was not *all*-knowing. Like God, he was powerful. Unlike God, he was not *all*-powerful. Like God, he had moral capabilities. But, unlike God, he did not know the difference between good and evil.

For a time, the relationship between God and man went along perfectly. Adam and Eve were content in their roles and were happy with their human limitations. Then Satan came to the Garden and things started to deteriorate. Satan suggested that God's order of things wasn't fair. He implied that God was holding out on Eve and that she didn't have to be content with being "just human." Neglecting the fact that God had created her with great beauty and intelligence and had given her dominion over the entire planet, Satan pointed out that she and Adam weren't equal to God. He reminded her that God knew some things that she didn't and that her knowledge wasn't unlimited.

The most vital decision in human history was then made. Eve's dilemma was, *Do I live out my life in the direction God built into me and be the apex of creation in dependence on Him? Or do I try to develop a different direction, one that might allow me to rule without any limitations whatsoever?* In other words, Eve had to choose whether she was going to accept her self and her position as it was, or if she was going to reject her self and her role and try to become like God.

Eve was fooled. She decided that the possibility of becoming like God was an attractive option. Under the impact of temptation, she apparently believed that she could improve on God's plan for her life. She was no longer content to live out her human role with its natural limitations. Giving in to the temptation, she took a bite of the forbidden fruit and then handed it to Adam.

In theological and psychological terms, Eve wanted to become omnipotent. She wanted to become all-knowing, all-wise, and all-powerful—just like God. She rejected her position as a child of God and tried to become His equal. This was the essence of her sin and disobedience.

Similarly, the essence of our sin today is our desire to be like God. *We* want to decide how intelligent we should be. *We* want to decide how attractive we should be. *We* want to decide how much financial prosperity we should achieve. *We* want to determine how our mates react. And *we* want to be in control. Just as a child who wants to grow up quickly and become like his giant parents, we want to be the ones who decide our destiny.

The problems this decision creates are endless. Like a child who is never satisfied because he isn't grown up yet or because he never reaches the fantasies of his youth, we are never satisfied. Since we have rejected ourselves as God designed us, we are trying to reach a totally unrealistic goal. Until we accept the fact that we have significant limitations, we can never be free to love ourselves. We will continue to struggle to achieve or develop toward some imaginary goal with the hope that, once we're there, we will be satisfied. We will be just like a child who is always wanting more and our selfish desires to become godlike will continue to wreak havoc with our self-esteem.

**Depression
and
Self-love**

9

Depression
and Self-love

Our society is experiencing an epidemic of depression. People everywhere are hounded by feelings of despondence and discouragement. Some, filled with depression and self-hatred, have turned to suicide—the ultimate solution. Others, suffering from less intense depression, live with daily thoughts of failure, inadequacy, and dissatisfaction with themselves. And nearly all of us occasionally get discouraged, down, or blue.

The severely depressed person is extremely self-critical, sensitive, and self-effacing. While he may put up an optimistic front, just beneath the surface lies an endless reservoir of guilt, condemnation, and self-contempt. Inadequacy and insecurity rule the day. He feels unloved and unlovable, and is filled with hatred for himself. He has high standards and expectations, but has given up all hope of reaching them since past efforts have done little to relieve his guilty conscience and nagging self-debasement.

Like all of us, the depressed person clings either to the ideals he learned from his parents or to his own unrealistic aspirations.

But instead of using his ideals as a goal or for motivation, he uses them to inflict punishment on himself. The depressed person's standards and expectations serve as a yardstick to measure his own self-punishment. Whenever he falls short of his extreme demands (which is most of the time), he punishes himself for not living up to his aspirations. Since depression is one of the major results of a lack of self-love, let's take a closer look at its beginnings.

The Origins of Depression

The early home environment of people suffering from depression typically reflects one or more of the following characteristics: (1) excessive guilt and pressure; (2) unrealistic expectations; (3) conditional acceptance; (4) lack of warmth and emotional support; or (5) emotional repression.

The person who suffers from depression lived with criticism, pressure, rejection, guilt, or shame as a child. No matter how hard he tried, his efforts never seemed to be good enough. Often his parents kept pressuring, nagging, shaming, or in some way challenging him to better things. At other times they just ignored him. In either case, the young child was left with the feeling that he could never please his parents or that he just wasn't that important to them. This produced the thought, *If I can't satisfy my parents, how can I ever love myself?*

Depression is a good example of what happens when people try to earn love through living up to others' expectations. For some reason the person who is susceptible to periods of depression has usually internalized a lofty set of standards from his parents. Failure to satisfy the expectations of his ideal self results in a loss of self-esteem.

At the same time this person was setting up these high expectations, he was also experiencing a lot of anger and frustration. Resisting the parental pressure that none of us appreciates, he wanted to be loved and accepted just the way he was. But a young child is often afraid to express the anger he feels toward his parents, since it might bring more guilt or rejection. So he learns to keep it in. Rather than saying, "I am angry with you for not giving me what I want or treating me the way I want to be treated," the depressed person learns to blame himself. He accepts his parents' criticism as reality, rather than challenging their perceptions. He learns to repress his anger and turn it on himself. And he develops a giant-sized set of self-punitive attitudes. Consequently, each time he falls short of his or others' standards, he punishes himself mentally. He thinks, *I'm no good,* or *Look how I mess things up,* or *How stupid of me!*

Later, as adults, many of us continue this childhood pattern of self-blame. Periodically, the combination of demanding standards and self-punitive attitudes rises up to attack our self-esteem. In fact, these feelings are sometimes so strong that they take away all energy and motivation, leaving us feeling futile and completely worthless.

In summary, depression grows out of childhood experiences that give rise to the three false assumptions that we looked at in chapter eight. We fall prey to depression because we believe that self-love and self-esteem have to be earned by pleasing others or by living up to our own desires. And we punish ourselves for failing to live up to these expectations. Our experiences with our parents have left us without the deep conviction that we are deeply loved and of immense worth just the way we are.

Depression also involves one other false assumption. We believe that since self-love is so hard to come by, there is really no use trying to gain it. We might as well give up. After years of only moderate success at pleasing our parents or others, some of us become depressed, lose hope, and settle into a pattern of discouragement and pessimism.

Although this process is extremely painful, it does have a few benefits. To begin with, if we give up hope, we won't be disappointed in the future. As long as we don't try, we cannot fail. Depression and self-punishment also have another benefit. If we punish or reject ourselves, we ward off possible rejection from other sources. If we say; "I'm horrible. I'm a failure. No one should love me," very few people will come along and say, "You're right. You certainly are a mess!" Instead, most will offer encouragement and support. Unfortunately, these temporary gestures of love and reassurance, also called secondary gains, are just hollow shells and do little for the depressed person's lasting sense of self-acceptance.

While the depressed person may give up trying to achieve his ideals in order to overcome conflict and to secure love, this is not the entire story. Remember how you reacted as a child when someone kept expecting too much of you? You tried your best, but it was never quite enough. Finally, after continued pressure and exhortation, you became frustrated and gave up. You thought, *I can never satisfy you no matter what I do so I quit!*

You quit, partly because you couldn't do it and partly because of the constant pressure. The only way to get your parent or teacher off your back was to quit, so you did. This was motivated partly by discouragement, but also by anger. Quitting was your way of getting even or rebelling.

The depressed person operates on this same principle. The only difference is that his quitting is no longer rebellion against an external authority figure. He rebelliously gives up in the face of his own internalized directives. He resents his own unrealistic standards, but cannot overcome them. He rebels against the constant pressures of his own ideals and turns the anger he once felt toward the authority figure against his personal expectations. His mind becomes a psychic battlefield occupied by a stern, coercive conscience and an apparently defeated but still stubbornly resistive child. Just as children frequently resist in the face of external pressures, the depressive person gives up and withdraws to gain temporary victory over his threatening ideals. In the process, of course, he reinforces his poor self-image. His ideals judge his passive rebellion and issue greater condemnation. What began as a way of avoiding feelings of failure and inadequacy ends up promoting these feelings.

The Strategy of Detachment

Some people take a slightly different turn in trying to solve their lack of self-acceptance. They attempt to resolve their conflicts by restricting their emotional awareness and by avoiding all lively feelings. Since they know meaningful involvement and intimacy may involve fear, rejection, or frustration, they start to put distance between themselves and others, while also avoiding their own emotions. Since they believe that setting their sights on meaningful achievements will only produce failure, they try not to set up any goals or expectations. These people won't allow themselves to become intimate—even in their marriage—because they fear the closeness. They are constantly on guard against their feelings, and their limited range of interests falls more into the areas of work, hobbies, or intellectual pursuits than into stimulating activities involving people. Often their interests fall into a dull routine that makes the person seem like a robot.

By avoiding contact, intimacy, and emotional involvement, these people attempt to choke off painful inner feelings. Seeking to avoid discouragement, depression, anxiety, and anger, they are willing to pay the price of an almost lifeless emotional existence. In fact, they often develop a proud superiority that looks down on people who are able to feel and love. A detached person may view these people as weak, vulnerable, and not to be admired, even though a part of him hungers to be involved with others. He is much like Captain Spock of "Star Trek." He is free from the frailties of feelings and therefore he can avoid problems with his self-esteem. But he also misses out on the excitement and fulfillment of God-given emotions.

Christianity and Self-love

In Christian circles, problems of depression and detachment are often compounded by negative experiences. Many churches, for example, emphasize man's sinfulness to such an extent that they overlook our great value and significance to God. In sermon after sermon, or experience after experience, we are told that we are sinful, wrong, or bad. These messages tend to undermine our self-acceptance, especially if we are already prone to feelings of self-rejection. In fact, there is an entire school of Christian thought built largely on the premise that we are no good and that it is sinful to like ourselves. Popular with those influenced by the Keswick Movement, followers of this school believe that we really don't possess any dignity or worth and that we should not like ourselves. "Since we are sinful and worthless," they argue, "we should give up all efforts to develop and to think positively about ourselves. In fact, we should find a way of bringing our own life to an end so that Christ's life can live through us." Here is one example:

> But dying to self is not a thing we do once for all. There may be an initial dying when God first shows these things, but ever after, it will be a constant dying, for only so can the Lord Jesus be revealed constantly through us. All day long the choice will be before us in a thousand ways. It will mean no plans, no time, no money, no pleasure of our own. It will mean a constant yielding to those around us, for our yielded- ness to God is measured by our yieldedness to man. Every humiliation, everyone who tries and vexes us, is God's way of breaking us, so that there is a yet deeper channel in us for the Life of Christ. You see, the only life that pleases God and that can be victorious is His life—never our life, no matter how hard we try. But inasmuch as our self-centered life is the exact opposite of His, we can never be filled with His life unless we are prepared for God to bring our life constantly to death. And in that we must cooperate by our moral choice.[1]

In this passage, we are exhorted to bring our lives to death. This thinking has crept into many areas of Christian living. A hymn writer, for example, says:

> Alas! And did my Saviour bleed?
> And did my Sovereign die?
> Would He devote that sacred head
> For such a worm as I?[2]

Another author writes:

> In every heart there is a cross and a throne and each is occupied. If Jesus is on the throne, ruling, self is on the cross, dying. But if self is being obeyed, and so is ruling, then it is on the throne. And self on the throne means that Jesus has been put on the cross.[3]

This view of life is degrading both to God and to man. In one instance, we are told to become worms for Jesus. In another, we are told to bring our life to death. These views are degrading to man because we become subhuman. We become worthless, hollow shells rather than free, creative personalities who can respond to God in love.

A friend recently told me of an encounter he had with a new convert to this crucifixion view of Christian living. One day my friend met this acquaintance on the streets of Denver and asked, "How are you?"

With a vacant stare, the man replied, "Oh, I'm dead!"

Somewhat taken back, my friend jokingly said, "Oh, that's too bad! How did it happen?"

The other fellow then stated, "Last night I died with Christ."

This is an extreme reaction and one that I suspect most advocates of self-crucifixion would reject. Nevertheless, it does illustrate (in an admittedly bizarre way) the logical conclusion of the school of self-crucifixion. If we take the proponents of this viewpoint literally, we are led to believe that the goal of Christian living is to remove the human element from the life of the believer. Since we are considered worthless, we are to bring our lives to an end so that the life of Jesus can flow through us.

This view is degrading to God because it pronounces His creation to be a total waste and implies that nothing can be done to renew our fallen lives. They are so worthless that they can only be replaced.

Proponents of this view take a few Scripture verses out of context, mix them with the truth of man's sinfulness, and come to the conclusion that it is somehow possible to bring an end to our life and substitute Christ's life in its place.

To people who are filled with feelings of failure and inadequacy, this teaching has strong appeal. No longer, they believe, will they have to struggle against inferiority and inadequacy. Instead, by acknowledging that they are absolutely worthless, they can become the recipient of something great—"Christ's life."

I appreciate their sincere goal. They want to overcome their sinfulness. But replacing their lives with God is not the way to do it. As we saw in chapter two, the Bible teaches that we should love ourselves. It does not teach that our ego, or self, is to be hated, crucified, done away with, or repressed. Instead, our ego is our total person, created in God's image and destined to spend eternity with Him. Proponents of the negative view of Christian living equate the ego with our sinfulness.

As one author puts it, "Self—the old sin nature—is also the object of His [God's] abhorrence and He yearns to rid us of its control and dominion by putting it to the cross of Christ."[4]

But this concept is false. The self is not the old sin nature. The self is our total person, created in God's image. God does not hate us and He does not yearn to put us to the cross of Christ. Christ has already gone to the cross for our sins.

This view only causes increased depression or detachment from ourselves and others. We end up considering ourselves worthless, mere physical containers for the life of another person, Christ. This teaching causes us to lose our own sense of uniqueness, individuality, and worth. "But," you say, "what about depravity? Doesn't the Bible teach that we are totally corrupted or depraved?" Much confusion has come from a misunderstanding of this concept.[5]

Some assume that if we are totally depraved we must be worthless, consequently we must berate or minimize ourselves. But this is far from the truth. The concept of depravity simply means that every area of our life is influenced and corrupted by sin. It means that our bodies are not as healthy as they should be. It means our minds are not functioning as they were intended. It means our emotions are influenced by sin. And it means that we are totally unable to earn God's acceptance through our efforts.

But depravity does not mean we are of no value, significance, or worth. There is a difference between a lack of righteousness or holiness on the one hand, and a lack of significance, worth, or value on the other. None of us have righteousness to commend ourselves to God, but we are of immense value and significance to Him. Sin destroys our righteousness, but it does not destroy our value or our worth to God. Our self-acceptance is rooted in the fact that we are created in God's image and no matter how deep our sin it cannot eradicate this image and destroy our significance to God.

Even though intellectually we see the problems with a self-crucifixion view of the Christian life, most of us have probably fallen prey to a little of this thinking. Let's say that you sing a solo or give a testimony at a Christian meeting. Afterward, when someone tells you that he appreciates your efforts, you probably felt a little uncomfortable. You may even have said, "It wasn't me. It was the Lord who did it through me." You detached yourself from your performance under the guise of humility. Since you felt uncomfortable with a compliment, you rejected the person's sincere appreciation.

If we are not careful, we can carry this to a most unfortunate conclusion. Any time we do something good, it is God who does it. But when we fail, it's either our fault (leading to depression) or the fault of our old nature or old man (leading to detachment). In either case, our personal wholeness is attacked. God gets all the credit. He is good but we are bad.

The truth of the matter is that God doesn't "sing through us." He creates us with the capacity to sing or speak and He redeemed us. But we respond to His love by practicing and developing our talent so that we can be a witness for Him. We need to acknowledge this dual responsibility and not minimize our own or God's responsibility. We need to reflect the twin facts that God is our Creator and that we as human beings are given the free choice to develop our abilities and commit them to Him or to let them lie dormant and therefore abuse them.

A better way of responding is to say, "Thank you. I really enjoy singing for the Lord." Another response is, "Thank you, I appreciate that."

The Fiction of Self-crucifixion

The self-crucifixion approach to establishing identity is a most unfortunate and unbiblical solution. In teaching that anything that comes from self is worthless, this approach to life minimizes or rejects our uniqueness and individuality. And in claiming that our life can be brought to death and supplanted with Christ's life, it attempts to turn us into religious robots.

One proponent of this view says that Christ causes *"to pass through us* such thoughts, such words, and such deeds as shall be always acceptable to God the Father when they are rightly presented to Him through Christ Jesus our Lord."[6] In other words, we have no thoughts or actions of our own. Our minds are put out of gear and Christ's thoughts run through us like water through a pipe. If this isn't sufficient degradation, the writer goes on to say that as the thoughts of God are passed through us, they become tainted like water passing through a dirty pipe. According to this view, the human being doesn't even make a decent bucket! The human race—created in God's image, given the responsibility of ruling over the earth, redeemed by Christ—is reduced to dirty pipe. We become mere nonbeings through whom God can work.

In addition to confusing the biblical meaning of ego, the self-crucifixion approach to personal identity is usually built on the inadequate interpretation of two Scripture passages: Romans 6:6 and Galatians 2:20.

> For we know that our old self was crucified with him so that the body of sin might be rendered powerless, that we should no longer be slaves to sin—(Rom. 6:6).

> I have been crucified with Christ and I no longer live, but Christ lives in me. The life I live in the body, I live by faith in the Son of God, who loved me and gave himself for me (Gal. 2:20).

Proponents of self-crucifixion believe that we must crucify either our self (or ego) or what they call "the old nature." This crucifixion is then followed by an infusion of Christ's life in us.

While this interpretation seems to be extremely spiritual, it has serious theological inadequacies. In addition to encouraging self-hatred and minimizing man's significance and worth, it misinterprets Scripture. The crucifixion mentioned in these passages does not refer to any present crucifixion of our self. In Romans 6:6, Paul uses the Greek aorist tense, which literally means "was crucified" (past tense). Newer versions of the Bible such as the New American Standard translate Romans 6:6 as, "Knowing this, that our old self *was* crucified with Him [italics added]." The tense of the verb here clearly indicates that Paul was referring to a past crucifixion, Christ's death on the cross, not something occurring in the present. Paul was referring to the fact that in a judicial sense we were crucified with Christ. In other words, when Christ died on the cross, He paid the legal penalty for all of our sins.

The same is true of Galatians 2:20. Paul writes this verse in a passage describing the past occurrence of our justification, not the current occurrence of our self-crucifixion. We read in verses 16-21:

> Know that a man is not *justified* by observing the law, but by faith in Jesus Christ. So we, too, have put our faith in Christ Jesus that we may be *justified* by faith in Christ and not by observing the law, because by observing the law no one will be *justified.*
>
> If, while we seek to be *justified* in Christ, it becomes evident that we ourselves are sinners, does that mean that Christ promotes sin? Absolutely not! If I rebuild what I destroyed, I prove that I am a lawbreaker. For through the law I died to the law so that I might live for God. I have been crucified with Christ and I no longer live, but Christ lives in me. The life I live in the body, I live by faith in the Son of God, who loved me and gave himself for me. I do not set aside the grace of God, for if righteousness could be gained through the law, Christ died for nothing! [italics added]

The context of Galatians 2:20 is a past, completed justification. In no way is Paul referring to a current, inner experience of crucifixion. He is saying that Christ paid for all our sins and that we now have new lives as Christians. He does not say that we lose our desires, our individuality, or our personality. He points out that we have become new creatures since our redemption (Col. 3:10). No longer living our lives apart from Christ, we now exist in vital fellowship with Him (John 15:1-14).

Although the adherents of self-crucifixion are sincere in their attempt to resolve their identity problem and overcome their sinfulness, their methods and basic perspectives are biblically unjustified and false. The way for us to escape our sinfulness is not to replace our lives with Christ. There is absolutely no spiritual or psychological way that we can bring our own life to an end.

Instead of misusing our Christianity to tear down our own and others' self-esteem, we need to clearly understand the great worth and value God has placed on us. A recent Christian song entitled "You're Something Special" does this extremely well.

> When Jesus sent you to us,
>   We loved you from the start;
> You were just a bit of sunshine
>   From heaven to our hearts.
> Not just another baby,
>   'Cause since the world began,
> There's been something very special
>   For you in His plan.
> That's why He made you special,
>   You're the only one of your kind,
> God gave you a body
>   And a bright healthy mind;
> He had a special purpose
>   That He wants you to find,
> So He made you something special,
>   You're the only one of your kind.

Notes

1. Roy Hession, *The Calvary Road* (Fort Washington, Pa.: Christian Literature Crusade, 1964), p. 16.
2. Isaac Watts, "Alas! And Did My Saviour Bleed?"
3. S. D. Gordon, *Quiet Talks on Prayer* (New York: Grosset and Dunlap, 1903), p. 109.
4. Charles Soloman, *Handbook of Happiness* (Denver: Grace Fellowship Press, 1971), p. 93.
5. For a good understanding of the concept of depravity, see A. H. Strong, *Systematic Theology* (Old Tappan, N. J.: Fleming H. Revell, 1907), pp. 637-644.
6. Quoted in *A New Call to Holiness*, J. Sidlow Baxter (Grand Rapids: Zondervan, 1973), p. 61.

Seeing Ourselves From God's Perspective

10
Seeing Ourselves From God's Perspective

While I was working on this book, I taught a class at our local church. For several Sundays, class members and I discussed the biblical basis for self-love and self-esteem. During one of those discussions, an attorney in his thirties raised his hand and asked, "But how can we learn to like ourselves? For years, I've been taught that self-love is a sin. It's great to hear that it isn't and to know that I can like myself. But I can't change overnight. It's one thing to know that I can like myself. It's another thing to do it!"

This statement triggered a lively discussion and some helpful interaction. One person suggested, "The first thing we've got to do is to know the Bible's teaching on self-love and self-acceptance." Another stated, "We just need to trust the Lord." A third said, "Trusting God sounds fine in principle, but I want to know how to apply it practically." "Even though I know that the Bible teaches self-love," another said, "I feel guilty whenever I think too positively about myself." Another responded, "It takes time to learn to like ourselves." And still another said, "We can't really learn to love ourselves unless we are loved by others."

Each of these people touched on certain aspects of the process of increasing our self-acceptance. But the variety of opinions reflects another truth. We can't suddenly change our lifelong attitudes by hearing that God wants us to love ourselves. Our attitude toward ourself has developed over many years and usually it doesn't change overnight.

So far we have a basic grasp of the self-esteem that God offers us. We also have some understanding of how our self-concept is formed during our early years of life and how certain experiences and patterns of thinking work against the process of building a positive self-concept. But now we need to learn what we can do to experience positive self-evaluation. How can we move from feelings of guilt, pressure, and self-dissatisfaction to the relaxed, loving, and affirming style of life that God intends us to have? I believe there are five basic steps we need to take in order to learn to love ourselves more fully. The first of these is the basis of all others—a commitment to seeing ourselves as God sees us.

The Divine Perspective

A short time ago, I traveled to the east coast for a two-day family seminar. During one of the half-hour breaks, a young woman named Lynn asked if she could speak to me. As we talked, I learned that her husband was in the Navy and was frequently at sea for lengthy periods.

After Lynn described her unbearable loneliness during these long separations, I asked, "Did this feeling begin after your marriage?"

"Oh, no!" she replied, and went on to describe her lifelong struggle with depression and feelings of being alone. Soon it became apparent to me that Lynn's problem was not simply her husband's frequent absence. His travels only triggered her underlying fears of self-rejection. She had a long history of rejection and inadequate self-love. Her father was a harsh disciplinarian. Her mother worked, and was seldom home while Lynn was growing up. At her church, known for its hellfire and brimstone preaching, Lynn was taught that she was sinful, but rarely heard about God's love. All of these factors combined to undercut her self-esteem. Although she was attractive, she didn't feel that way. And although she was likeable, she couldn't really believe that others liked her.

Since our time was growing short, I listened for a while longer and made a few suggestions. I encouraged Lynn to share her feelings with her husband. I suggested that she develop a few close friends. I also told her that professional counseling would be helpful if her negative attitudes persisted. She seemed open to each of these suggestions. Then I said, "All of these are ways of reaching a very basic goal. You need to learn to really like yourself. If you are ever going to overcome your feelings of loneliness, you will have to make creating a strong self-image one of the highest priorities in your life."

Lynn looked at me sadly and said, "Dr. Narramore, I want to learn to love myself more than you will ever know. But it doesn't seem like the right thing to do. Aren't we to 'seek first the kingdom of God'? It seems awfully selfish to give so much attention to myself."

Lynn was sincere about her marriage and about her Christian faith. And she really wanted to develop a better attitude toward herself. But when I suggested that she make self-love a high priority, she immediately revealed how deep down her self-rejection went. Although she wanted to feel good about herself, such feelings seemed wrong. Deep within her personality, the years of rejection, loneliness, and distorted teaching rose up to tell her that she should not love herself. My statement was more than she could handle. She thought that self-acceptance might be okay as a by-product of loving God, but a specific goal of learning to love herself was not acceptable.

Many of us are like Lynn. We want to develop a more positive attitude toward ourselves, but this doesn't seem quite right. To set a goal of learning to love ourselves seems entirely out of line. Yet this is exactly what we need. Putting a priority on self-acceptance is the first step many of us need to take if we are going to build a more positive attitude toward ourselves. We must stop relegating ourselves and our personal growth to second-level status, and realize that such attitudes are not within God's plan for us.

It is curious that when we have a bad attitude toward another person, we can usually acknowledge our sinfulness and decide to change. That person, we know, is created in God's image and deserves our love and esteem. But when we harbor an attitude of self-rejection, we sometimes feel that this is acceptable. Perhaps we are afraid to love ourselves because we fear that we will selfishly put ourselves ahead of God and others. Or maybe we think that we will become proud, self-centered, or arrogant. But as we saw earlier, biblical self-love is not arrogant, proud, or selfish. Instead, it leads to greater respect and love for ourselves and others.

Setting a high priority on self-acceptance actually means committing ourselves to the truth of God's estimation of us. It means acknowledging both our strengths and weaknesses. It means believing that we are created by God and redeemed by Christ. And what could possibly be wrong with that?

Only when we develop a balanced perception of who we are can we function the way that God intends. We must start by seeing ourselves as creations of the living God. That's one reason why, when God first told us about the human race, He emphasized that we are created in His image. Throughout Scripture, we are told that we are significant yet sinful. When we focus on our sins at the expense of our significance, we are actually committing another sin. We are denying the value of God's creation and rejecting His evaluation of us. We must begin where God begins, with man being made in His image. Until we recognize the truth of our significance, we cannot deal meaningfully with the problem of our sin and our redemption makes no sense.

At this point, a word of caution is in order. In setting a priority on the development of biblical self-love, I am not saying that self-love is the most important thing in the world, and I am not implying that self-love is an end in itself. *Self-love is only one aspect of a total world view that includes a proper set of attitudes toward God, ourselves, and others.* Toward God, we need a true perception of His holiness, justice, love, and goodness. Toward ourselves and others, we need a balanced understanding of our significance and worth, on the one hand, and our sinfulness on the other. I am stressing self-love here because the church too frequently has ignored this side of the biblical view of man. Focusing on man's sinfulness in order to demonstrate his need of redemption, the church has overlooked the fact that God has created man in His image.

When I talk about biblical self-love, I am not describing a short-term, worldly view of happiness. Happiness is not the only (or even the most important) goal in life. Too many people in our culture are on a happiness kick and haven't realized that happiness isn't all there is to life. When I discuss self-love, I am talking about how we can learn to accept God's total evaluation of us. This is exceedingly important, since our attitude toward ourselves influences the quality of our relationships with God and others. In fact, our attitude toward ourselves is a major factor in determining the type of attitude we have toward God.

Self-love and God's Love

A recent study of over one hundred Christian high school students demonstrated the intimate connection between our love for ourselves and our perception of God's love. Two researchers evaluated the students' attitude toward themselves—their self-concept—and their perception of God. The results were exceedingly significant. Students who had the highest level of self-esteem viewed God as loving and kind, while students who had a poor image of themselves tended to see God as vindictive, stern, angry, controlling, and impersonal. Apparently the students' attitudes toward themselves influenced the way they viewed God.[1]

I had a classic experience with this not long ago. A minister in his mid-40s came to our clinic for counseling, suffering from depression and the belief that he had failed in the ministry. As counseling progressed, he confessed that he had a terrible lack of confidence, including uncertainty about his salvation. "I have been a pastor for twenty years," he said, "and have shown many people the way to God through Christ. I think that I love the Lord and I want to do His will. But when I get in these moods, I just don't think that I'm saved." The pastor went on to discuss his extensive theological education (a doctorate from a well-known seminary) and the fact that he was thoroughly committed to a traditional Calvinistic view of eternal security, which says that a Christian can never lose his salvation. He could quote biblical passages such as: "My sheep hear My voice, and I know them, and they follow Me; and I give eternal life to them, and they shall never perish; and no one shall snatch them out of my hand" (John 10:27-28 NASB). He had even preached sermons on the security of the child of God. But every time he became depressed, he questioned his salvation. He would think, *I'm no good. I'm a failure. Therefore God cannot possibly love me.* His emotions and his own self-rejection forced him to assume that God could not accept him.

For weeks, this pastor struggled with his problem. He discussed some of his sins that had caused tremendous guilt. He looked at the loneliness he had felt as a child, remembering his father's temper and how petrified he had been when his dad went out of control. Gradually, he began to see the source of his spiritual insecurity; he felt unloved by his father. Although he "knew" (intellectually) that God loved him, he couldn't believe it during periods of depression. As he developed a better attitude toward himself and his earthly father, he began to overcome his intense fear of losing his salvation. Biblical passages he had known intellectually for years suddenly came to life. As he learned to love himself, he grew to love God more and became confident that God loved him and wasn't going to cast him off in a fit of anger.

This illustration and the study on high school students both demonstrate the importance of a proper attitude toward ourselves. Our self-concept actually influences our concept of God. As long as we have a bad attitude toward ourself, we will tend to distort biblical teachings on who God is. But the influence of our self-concept doesn't end there. It also influences our relationships with others.

Self-love and Loving Others

According to the Bible, we are to love others as ourselves (Luke 10:27), and as God loves us (John 4:11). In other words, there is an intimate connection between our love for ourselves and our love and esteem for God and others. When we fail to love ourselves, all of our relationships suffer. We fail to love our mates, our children, or our neighbors properly. Think of your own life. Remember the last time you were feeling miserable and were angry with yourself, discouraged, or depressed? How did you relate to your mate, children, and friends at that time? Were you loving, sensitive, and kind? I doubt it. When we are uptight about ourselves, we are usually uptight with others. We take our frustrations out on them.

When we fail to love ourselves as God intended, we create one of two problems in our relationship with our family. We either try to compensate for our feelings of inadequacy by denying our faults and blaming others, or we derogate ourselves. When we elevate ourselves above others—minimizing their worth and value, blaming them unfairly—we commit the sin of pride. When we place ourselves below them, we minimize *our* worth and value. In either case, we are in trouble, for we are hurting ourselves and others, and also debasing one of God's creations.

The following chart shows what happens when we evaluate ourselves poorly. It shows that what we commonly think of as pride usually stems from a negative self-image, and that a very low opinion of ourselves is actually a reverse form of pride.

	Conscious Attitude Toward Oneself	Unconscious Attitude Toward Oneself	Who Gets the Glory
Pride	Superiority	Inferiority	Self
False Humility	Inferiority	Superiority	Self
True Humility	Respect, self-acceptance, and an awareness of our sinfulness	Respect, self-acceptance, and an awareness of our sinfulness	God

Pride and Confidence

A proud person's conscious attitude toward himself is one of superiority. He goes through life focusing on his successes and comparing himself favorably to others. Underneath, however, we find a very different state of affairs. The person who constantly focuses on his greatness is actually struggling unsuccessfully to ward off deep feelings of inferiority.

A confident person, on the other hand, doesn't have to compare himself to others or elevate himself above them to support a sagging self-esteem. He can focus on the strengths of others, being flexible and truly humble. He knows the truth of the apostle Paul's writings. "Let everyone be sure that he is doing his very best," Paul writes, "for he will have the personal satisfaction of work well done, and won't need to compare himself with someone else" (Gal. 6:4 LB).

True and False Humility

The attitudes of the person with false humility are the opposite of those of the proud person. On the surface, a person with false humility seems to be extremely humble. He focuses on his weaknesses and failures, accentuating the negative aspects of his life, and has great difficulty believing that God can love and forgive him. He knows the Bible's teachings on forgiveness, but for some reason he can't apply them to himself. He may believe that God can forgive a Hitler, a murderer, or a rapist, but he somehow feels that his sins are beyond forgiveness. At first glance, these attitudes seem to be extremely humble and self-effacing. But we see that things are not what they seem when we look deeper.

When we look below the surface, we see that inferiority is a reverse form of pride. The person with false humility—usually someone with a poor self-concept—has an exalted image of his badness. He criticizes himself for every thought and action, exaggerating his faults to unbelievable proportions. Instead of accepting God's forgiveness, he says, "My badness is greater [or stronger] than God's goodness. Christ's death may have paid the penalty for others' sins, but it won't take care of mine." Such people elevate the strength of their sinfulness far above

God's estimation of it. They make their sins seem so bad that they negate the entire purpose of Christ's death on the cross. In essence, they are denying the value of Christ's atonement.

In contrast to the proud person's underlying feelings of inferiority and the "humble" person's grandiose exaggerations of sinfulness, the truly humble person has a balanced attitude toward himself. He knows that he is highly significant to God and that he can possess a strong sense of self-esteem and self-acceptance. At the same time, he also knows his sinfulness and failures. This perspective allows him to maintain a balanced self-image. He does not resort to either proud overexaggerations of his capabilities or degrading underestimations of his worth. Consequently, he can live life with confidence and humility. He is able to lovingly serve others out of an awareness of their worth and value. Ultimately, such a perspective naturally leads to the glorification of God, the Designer and Redeemer of the human personality.

Summary

Self-love is not a narcissistic or self-centered goal. It is a central part of seeing ourselves as God sees us. We should learn to value ourselves, both because God values us and because we will then be able to love God and others more. This, then, is the first step in learning to love ourselves. We must make a commitment to seeing ourselves as God sees us. We must acknowledge to ourselves, *God, You have made me in Your image and made me to live eternally with You. Like Adam and Eve and all other members of the human race, I have sinned and marred that image. But Christ has paid the penalty for my sins. I know that You want me to recognize these facts. I know that You want me to lovingly respect myself and every other member of the human race.*

Notes

1. Peter Benson and Bernard Spilka, "God Image as a Function of Self-Esteem and Loss of Control," *Journal for the Scientific Study of Religion* 12 (1973): 297-310.

**A Biblical
Self-concept**

11

A Biblical
Self-concept

Once we are committed to seeing ourselves from God's perspective, we need to apply this commitment in a practical and comprehensive manner to our own self-concept. It is one thing to understand that we can love ourselves. It is another to apply this understanding to the specific situation and self-evaluation that we all must face. In this chapter, we will look at how we can apply the principle of self-love to some of our specific emotional needs. We will be looking at God's comprehensive provision for all aspects of our self-concept.

Psychologists generally agree that our self-image is made up of a number of thoughts and attitudes toward ourselves. We tend to think of ourselves as either competent or incompetent, lovable or unlovable, secure or insecure, worthy or unworthy. These attitudes vary from time to time, in relation to our performance and our own and others' evaluations of us. If we are doing well at school, home, or work, our self-confidence gets a shot in the arm. We walk a little taller and feel a little better about ourselves. If, however, we are doing poorly, the opposite takes place. We become a little insecure and our confidence begins to sag. Similarly, if people praise us or our achievements, we feel better about ourselves. If they criticize or rebuff us, our confidence takes a beating. In other words, the portion of our self-image relating to confidence can become a little shaky.

There are four central ingredients in our self-image: (1) a sense of worth; (2) confidence; (3) security; and (4) love. The first of these, a sense of dignity or worth is the basic attitude about our significance or value. If we are aware of our worth, we are on the road to a strong inner sense of identity. We believe we are significant. We believe we are valuable and that we have a right to live. Without a sense of worth, we become discouraged or depressed and fall prey to feelings of guilt, worthlessness, and condemnation.

A second ingredient in our self-concept is an attitude of confidence. Confidence, which implies a basic level of trust in our abilities and a sense of inner strength, is the quality that enables us to reach out and try new tasks or tackle new challenges. It is the opposite of inferiority. When confidence is lacking, we feel tense, anxious, frightened, or insecure.

Closely tied to a feeling of confidence is our need for a feeling of security. Whereas confidence is more of an internal matter ("I can do it!"), security is more external ("Others can be trusted." or "The world is safe."). Security relates to our environment and our relationship to it. It reflects our assurance that the world "out there" is basically safe. We needn't fear an impending earthquake, financial disaster, abandonment, or attack. This doesn't mean that the world is always a beautiful place or that everyone can be trusted. But it means that we have had sufficient positive experiences with others to know that we do have friends we can depend on, that the whole world isn't bad, and that we don't need to live in constant fear of starvation, physical disaster, or some other impending doom. People without a sense of security are constantly worrying about these and other potential tragedies and are unable to feel comfortable and relaxed.

A final ingredient in our self-concept is the feeling of being loved. Perhaps more than any other, this is the central ingredient of a positive attitude about ourselves. If we are to be happy and go through life with a minimum of problems, we need an assurance that we are loved and accepted and that we belong. When this is lacking, we feel alone, isolated, and depressed.

Conditional Self-concepts

As we have seen in earlier chapters, our self-concept begins to be formed in infancy. If our parents valued and accepted us, we developed a healthy sense of worth. If they complimented us and encouraged us to try new things, we gained a sense of confidence. If they provided a stable and secure environment, we learned to feel secure. And if they loved us freely, we learned to love ourselves.

On the other hand, if our parents had difficulty tolerating our weaknesses, this also affected our self-concept. If they were critical, easily frustrated, overprotective, or failed to communicate their deep sense of respect and love for us, we probably entered adulthood with mixed feelings about ourselves.

Human nature being what it is, no one enters adulthood with a totally healthy self-image. Every parent occasionally loses his temper and verbally attacks his child's sense of worth or undermines his feelings of security. Every parent occasionally criticizes, overprotects, or in some way undermines his child's developing sense of confidence.

These facts, coupled with our failure to live up to our own goals and expectations, mean that we all enter adulthood with a *relative* or *conditional* self-concept. Either our self-concepts are relative to our achievements and the recognition they bring or they are conditional—dependent on our achievements and the evaluations we receive from our parents and other significant people.[1] We learn to accept ourselves *if* we are able to live up to certain expectations, and we learn not to accept ourselves unless others *accept* us.

Such a perspective affects our whole style of living. Using the sentence "I can like myself *if* . . ." as our given, we go on to complete the sentence with any number of things. "I can like myself if I am successful." "I can like myself if I am likeable." "I can like myself if I am talented." "I can like myself if I am a good parent." "I can like myself if I am a good Christian."

But we can never fully succeed in living up to these conditions of acceptance. As children, we were able to please our parents some of the time. We were able to please our teachers some of the time. And we were able to please ourselves some of the time. Even as adults, we like ourselves and feel worthy, confident, secure, and loved some of the time. But at other times, serious doubts about our significance and worth arise. Our self-criticism, based on the conditional acceptance we received in our formative years, catches up with us and we become dissatisfied with ourselves when our performance slips or we don't gain the emotional support we want.

This shifting foundation for self-esteem can have serious consequences, for unless we live up to our inner expectations, we cannot really be content with ourselves. And even when we are content, we can't feel totally at ease because we know that our performance could slip and our self-doubt and self-criticism would return. As Maurice Wagner puts it:

> Our self-concept may seem fairly stable when life's ebb and flow of problems stays within acceptable limits. Occasionally, however, a tidal wave of unexpected difficulties overwhelms us. It may be a surprise illness, the sudden death of a loved one, a business failure, or a marriage or family problem that we cannot handle. Our boat is about to split in the middle and take water. At these times of unusual stress we become conscious of how strong or how weak our inner security really is. We seem to get in touch with our inner selves best in times of crisis. It is then that we begin to reach desperately for some resource to hold onto, some relationship that is available and reliable.[2]

An Unconditional Self-concept

The only absolutely sure and safe foundation on which we can build our self-esteem is a knowledge of ourself in relationship to God. He is absolute and unchanging in character. While human values shift and sway and many things on earth change, God remains a solid source of identity. The Bible says, "In the beginning, O Lord, you laid the foundations of the earth, and the heavens are the work of your hands. They will perish, but you remain; they will all wear out like a garment. You will roll them up like a robe; like a garment they will be changed. But you remain the same, and your years will never end" (Heb. 1:10-12).

This is one truth we can know. We can build our lives around the fact that God is God; what He promised, He will do. From this foundation, we can erect a strong and stable sense of personal identity. Our self-image does not have to rest on the shifting sand of our performance and it does not have to rely on the judgments and evaluations we receive from others. God takes care of the needs that arise from our self-concept.

We Are Worthy

Long before we ever experienced the impact of conditional acceptance or knew what it was like to fail and not like ourselves, God built into our genes a wonderful pattern for growth, fulfillment, and development. This God-given potential is the ultimate basis for self-esteem. With these carefully chosen words, David expresses God's ultimate foundation for our sense of value, significance, and worth:

> For Thou didst form my inward parts; Thou didst weave me in my mother's womb. I will give thanks to Thee, for I am fearfully and wonderfully made; wonderful are Thy works, and my soul knows it very well. My frame was not hidden from Thee, when I was made in secret, and skillfully wrought in the depths of the earth. Thine eyes have seen my unformed substance; and in Thy book they were all written, the days that were ordained for me, when as yet there was not one of them. How precious also are Thy thoughts to me, O God! How vast is the sum of them! If I should count them, they would outnumber the sand. When I awake, I am still with Thee (Ps. 139:13-18).

The infant in the crib is a product of God's handiwork. Although marred by sin, the design passed down through his genetic structure is straight from the hand of God. Made in God's image, according to His design, the infant has a wonderful, complex potential for physical, intellectual, spiritual, and social development.

We Are Competent

Next to the knowledge that God created us stands another pillar of our self-esteem—the awareness of our abilities and a sense of inner strength. This pillar speaks directly to our need for confidence, it is the knowledge that God gives unique talents to each of us. No two people are exactly alike. Yet every person who has ever walked the face of this earth has been given gifts by God. Paul puts it this way:

> Now God gives us many kinds of special abilities, but it is the same Holy Spirit who is the source of them all. There are different kinds of service to God, but it is the same Lord we are serving. There are many ways in which God works in our lives, but it is the same God who does the work in and through all of us who are his. The Holy Spirit displays God's power through each of us as a means of helping the entire church (1 Cor. 12:4-7 LB).

In a unique way, each of us has a broad range of capacities, attributes, and potential. While differing widely in the way our gifts fit together, we each possess a beautiful, complex arrangement of capabilities that forms the nucleus of our *real self*—the person God designs and intends us to be.

The apostle Paul again speaks of these capabilities when he writes, "We will in all things grow up into him who is the Head, that is, Christ. From him the whole body, joined and held together by every supporting ligament, grows and builds itself up in love, as each part does its work" (Eph. 4:15-16).

Sometimes we forget this powerful truth and feel tense, anxious, frightened, or insecure. We focus so much on our weaknesses and failures that we forget our talents and gifts. But if we remember God's creation, we gain a truer realization of the talents we possess. This gives us a solid basis for a sense of confidence. A recent children's chorus, "I Am a Promise," puts it well:

> I am a promise;
>   I am a possibility;
> I am a promise with a capital P
>   I can be anything, anything God wants me to be.

How true it is that we are a promise with a capital *P*. The God of the universe built that promise into the fabric of our being. The fact that God has given us gifts and the power to use them is an absolute and unshakable foundation for our confidence. If we are merely chance beings with no special origin or abilities, we would have to struggle continuously to find confidence and to demonstrate our talents.

But now we can be at peace. We can rest in the complete confidence that whatever God intends that we should do, He has given us the ability to accomplish. We can confidently reach out, trying new ideas and tackling new challenges. Paul writes, "I can do everything through him who gives me strength" (Phil. 4:13). And Christ says, "I am the vine; you are the branches. If a man remains in me and I in him, he will bear much fruit . . ." (John 15:5).

We Are Secure

The third ingredient, our need for a feeling of security, is closely tied to a feeling of confidence. Here again, Scripture lays out a rich and trustworthy provision.

Do you remember the 1972 Olympics in Munich, Germany, in which several Arab guerillas held five Israelis hostage? For hours, the world waited anxiously for word about the captives. Finally it came: "They have all been murdered."

I will never forget the shock on the faces of the television newsmen. They sat in silent disbelief. Finally, after a long pause, one of them said, "There's nothing we can say at a time like this." Then he went on to indicate that we could only "hope and pray" that things would get better.

My son, Dickie, and I were watching that telecast together. We were both deeply touched at the tragic loss of life and the seemingly senseless conflict. But then, we discussed the situation. I shared with Dickie the origin of the Arab and Israeli nations and explained that Ishmael, the son of Abraham by his wife's maid, Hagar, was the father of the Arab people. Then we discussed the spread of the Israelites throughout the world and their eventual return to the Promised Land. I showed Dickie from the Bible that the current Arab-Israeli conflict is part of a centuries-long problem that will eventually culminate in the return of Christ to earth. I told him that these conflicts weren't going to cease; they would probably get worse. But in the end, God's plans would triumph. This biblical insight helped us to put the whole event into proper perspective and provided needed security during those troubled days.

In similar ways, the Bible sheds light on numerous perplexing events and happenings of our day. It is our one great source of security in the midst of the confusing happenings in our world. God promises us security in our relationship to Him. He promises that nothing will be able to separate us from His love (Rom. 8:38-39). He is with us day by day and we will spend eternity with Him.

We Are Loved

The final ingredient in our self-concept is the feeling of being loved. Probably the best-known verse in the New Testament is John 3:16, which reads, "For God so loved the world that he gave his one and only Son, that whoever believes in him shall not perish but have everlasting life." Here, in a nutshell, is the best foundation for a lasting attitude of self-love. Even before we were born, God chose us to be His children. The apostle Paul writes, "For he chose us in him before the creation of the world to be holy and blameless in his sight. In love he predestined us to be adopted as sons through Jesus Christ, in accordance with his pleasure and will" (Eph. 1:4-5).

Just as the fact that God created us with unique gifts can provide us with a deep, abiding sense of worth and confidence, the fact that God loves and chose us can provide a lasting source of assurance. What a strong foundation for self-acceptance we have, because God has chosen us to be His sons! This acceptance doesn't come and go according to our performance. It is a love that is completely unconditional. As David puts it:

> Where can I go from Thy Spirit? Or where can I flee from
> Thy presence? If I ascend to heaven, Thou art there; if I
> make my bed in Sheol, behold, Thou art there. If I take the

wings of the dawn, if I dwell in the remotest part of the sea, even there Thy hand will lead me, and Thy right hand will lay hold of me. If I say, "Surely the darkness will overwhelm me, and the light around me will be night," even the darkness is not dark to Thee, and the night is as bright as the day. Darkness and light are alike *to Thee* (Ps. 139:7-12).

God's love is unconditional. No matter where we go or how we do, God's love for us remains consistent. He is always present with us.

When the four ingredients of the positive self-concept are lacking, we suffer from the influence of an inadequate self-concept. Since each area of our self-concept has an opposite, we experience a negative emotion for every positive attitude that is missing. The ingredients in these two self-concepts, then, are:

Positive Self-concept	Negative Self-concept
Sense of Significance and Worth	Feeling of Badness, Worthlessness
Attitude of Confidence	Anxiety and Feelings of Inferiority
Feelings of Security	Insecurity and Worry
Awareness of Being Loved	Loneliness, Isolation, and Depression

The Christian's Choice

Now we can see that there are two possible directions for us as we attempt to establish self-esteem. The first direction says: "I can like myself *if* others like me." "I can like myself *if* I live up to my goals and expectations." "I can like myself *if* I succeed in avoiding feelings of guilt and condemnation." In other words, we can choose to build our self-love and self-acceptance on our performance and others' evaluations of us. *We can decide to operate on the basis of a conditional or relative self-concept.*

The problems with such an approach are obvious. Constantly

under pressure to perform, we must earn our acceptance. We must prove our worth and we must succeed in order to develop confidence. We must keep on looking for security. Although this is the approach we all use to some degree, it is an inadequate approach to self-acceptance.

By contrast, we can decide to establish our self-concept on the absolute and unchanging God of the universe. With Him, our worth is not conditional. We don't have to work to prove our competence or do anything to merit love, for our security is rooted in Him.

The first approach attempts to earn self-esteem through works. The second approach is based on God's grace. The first is built on comparison and competition. The second is available to all. How can we ever have a strong and lasting sense of self-esteem if it is dependent on our achievements and acceptance? If we judge ourselves on the basis of performance, one half of the people are destined to be losers. They can never measure up. But God didn't design this type of system. In God's system, everyone is entitled to dignity and worth. We are entitled to confidence and strength. We are all entitled to a feeling of security and lasting love. And it is God who provides for our needs of worth, confidence, security, and love.

Theology and Self-love

Since concepts of self-love and a positive self-image are still new in many Christian circles, I would like to briefly tie these concepts into a broader theological perspective. As we will see, the Christian's right to a sense of self-esteem is not an isolated teaching. Rather, it is a consistent theme that runs throughout biblical revelation.

Christian theologians have frequently divided their study of systematic theology into several basic categories. These areas are: (1) Theology proper: the study of God; (2) Anthropology: the study of man; (3) Soteriology: the study of salvation; (4) Pneumatology: the study of the Holy Spirit; (5) Eschatology: the study of end times; and (6) Ecclesiology: the study of the church. In each area, theologians have attempted to pull together in a systematic manner all the biblical data that relate to that topic. A brief look at these categories will demonstrate their relevance to the Christian's self-esteem.

Theology proper groups together all the biblical teachings on the nature, decrees, attributes, and works of God. In laying out the biblical truths of creation, this branch of theology provides a major foundation for a sense of self-esteem. Listen to a theologian writing over seventy years ago, long before psychologists started speaking about self-esteem and worth:

> *Christ's death for man, by showing the worth of humanity, has recreated ethics.* Plato defended infanticide as under certain circumstances permissible. Aristotle viewed slavery as founded in the nature of things. The reason assigned was the essential inferiority of nature on the part of the enslaved. But *the divine image in man makes these barbarities no longer possible to us. Christ sometimes looked upon men with anger, but he never looked upon them with contempt.* He taught the woman, he blessed the child, he cleansed the leper, he raised the dead. . . . Robert Burns, walking with a nobleman in Edinburgh, met an old townsfellow from Ayr and stopped to talk with him. The nobleman, kept waiting, grew restive, and afterward reproved Burns for talking to a man with so bad a coat. Burns replied, "I was not talking to the coat,—I was talking to the man."[3] [italics added]

What a clear statement of the worth of man! Since we are created in the image of God, we should see ourselves as significant and gifted.

Biblical Anthropology (the study of the nature of man) also addresses man's dignity and worth. It demonstrates the essential aspects of our nature, the meaning of the likeness of God, and the effect of sin on our lives.

Soteriology (the study of salvation) sheds further light on our right to self-esteem. In His great act of redemption, Christ restored alienated man to a position of sonship and fellowship with Him. This great expression of love speaks clearly to our value and significance to God. Christ Himself said, "For this reason I was born . . ." (John 18:37). The great doctrine of justification, which describes our restoration to God through the satisfaction of

Christ's death and the imputing of His righteousness to us, provides a sense of worth and love that surpasses anything the secular world can offer. As the apostle Paul puts it, "Therefore, since we have been justified through faith, we have peace with God through our Lord Jesus Christ" (Rom. 5:1). Our sins are paid and God looks on us as having all the righteousness of Christ Himself. "Therefore, there is now no condemnation for those who are in Christ Jesus" (Rom. 8:1).

Pneumatology (the study of the Holy Spirit) speaks both to our confidence and to our security. The Bible teaches that the Holy Spirit indwells us and that His work includes establishing the security of our relationship with God and empowering us to do God's work. 1 Corinthians 3:16 reads, "Don't you know that you yourselves are God's temple and that God's Spirit lives in you?" Ephesians says that our salvation was "sealed in Him [Christ] with the Holy Spirit of promise, who is given as a pledge of our inheritance, with a vew to the redemption of *God's own* possession, to the praise of His glory" (1:13-14 NASB).

Eschatology (the study of end times and future things) speaks to our worth, our sense of being loved, and to our security. The entire Book of Revelation and vast other sections of Scripture speak in depth about the future of mankind. God has prepared an eternity for His children and He is going to spend it with them.

Ecclesiology (the study of the church and the relationships between its members) speaks clearly to our need for love, security, confidence, and worth. Christ commands us to love one another. "Love one another. As I have loved you, so you must love one another" (John 13:34). The deep personal commitments that Christ calls His church to experience all relate to meeting the spiritual, physical, and emotional needs of other Christians.

All of these areas of theology, then, speak directly to the problem of man's self-concept. The basis and need for a positive self-concept is not at all a twentieth-century psychological phenomenon. It is deeply rooted in the fabric of divine revelation and is one of the greatest themes of Scripture. While this theme has not been consistently expounded by theologians, it has always been there and we can no longer choose to deny this vital message. God's whole plan for mankind is built on the assumption that we are significant to Him. We must let these thoughts sink deep into our minds if we are to experience all the rich rewards He has for us. We must recognize the *comprehensiveness* of God's provisions for our emotional needs.

Rather than simply memorizing Scripture or reciting doctrine, we need to realize that God is speaking directly to us about our personal needs, as well as to relationships with Him and others. When we approach Scripture with this in mind, we will find a wealth of God's revelations that speak to our need for security, worth, confidence, and love. And we will find that our self-concept is increasingly transformed from a relative and changing image to the firm, stable, and unconditional identity that is rooted in God's relationship to man.

Notes

1. I am indebted to Dr. Maurice Wagner for the concept of absolute and relative self-concepts.
2. Maurice Wagner, *The Sensation of Being Somebody* (Grand Rapids: Zondervan, 1976), p. 103.
3. A. H. Strong, *Systematic Theology* (Old Tappan, N. J.: Fleming H. Revell, 1907), p. 516.

**Giving Up
Your Guilt**

12

Giving Up Your Guilt

Deeply embedded in our personality is another process that rises up to challenge our positive attitudes of self-acceptance. This process, the voice of conscience and the emotion we know as guilt, steps in to undermine our positive evaluation just when we begin to feel better about ourselves. Guilt, the source of most of our negative self-evaluation, is the biggest barrier to self-esteem, and it keeps us in fear of punishment or rejection. In fact, if it weren't for guilt, we would have few problems with self-esteem.

Guilt and the Ideal Self

As we saw in chapter seven, guilt is triggered whenever our attitudes or actions fall below our expectations. Let's review the way guilt works, beginning with the standards, goals, or expectations that make up our ideal self.

These ideals are the first ingredients in our process of self-evaluation. They are our guidelines for self-judgment, and they come from several sources. Some are learned from our parents and peers. Others come from our own desires and wishes. And some are universal standards that God builds into the heart of every person. Whatever their source, these ideals come together to form a vital part of our personality, and they determine our hopes, our goals, our standards, and our expectations.

These ideals can be very beneficial. They give us an image of what we can become and in that way help to stimulate our growth. But frequently we misuse them. We set out after all kinds of things that really aren't ideal. We confuse our parents' standards or our own demands with the goals of God, or think that our every inner wish or urge is good. When this perspective develops, our ideals can turn against us, becoming vehicles for self-punishment rather than stimuli for growth.

Guilt and Conscience

The second ingredient in our process of self-evaluation is our conscience. Many of us think that conscience is a complete moral system. We believe that conscience includes our values, our awareness of our failures, and the guilt we experience after we have fallen short. But this is not the biblical view. Paul writes, "For when Gentiles who do not have the Law do instinctively the things of the Law, these, not having the Law, are a law to themselves, in that they show the work of the Law written in their hearts, their conscience bearing witness, and their thoughts alternately accusing or else defending them" (Rom. 2:14-15 NASB).

In this passage, Paul distinguishes between the law written in the heart, the conscience, and the thoughts that accuse or excuse. Biblically, the conscience is different from both the law (standards of perfection) and the accusing thoughts. Conscience is literally a co-knowledge. It is a knowledge of oneself in relation to a standard, the part of our psychic makeup that makes us aware of the gap between our expectations and our performance. It is the end result of Adam and Eve's search to "be like God, knowing good and evil" (Gen. 3:5).

Guilt and Our Thoughts

The third element in our process of self-evaluation is our thoughts. In chapter seven, we saw that we can experience two general types of thoughts and emotional reactions when we fall short of our standards. One consists of our fears of punishment, rejection, and loss of self-esteem. I have called this our punitive self. The other is the love-motivated, corrective attitude that I call constructive, or godly, sorrow.

Most people falsely equate the thoughts and emotions coming from their punitive self with conscience. They believe that the condemning guilt feelings that periodically rise up to attack their self-acceptance are the voice of conscience. But according to Paul, there is a difference between conscience and accusing thoughts.

I, too, used to believe that my accusing thoughts were the voice of God coming through my conscience. Conscience, I believed, was created by God to make people feel guilty so that they would be motivated to live better lives. As a child, when I disobeyed my parents or harbored sinful thoughts or actions, I assumed that the guilt I felt was God speaking to me about my sin.

Then, a few years ago, I decided to undertake a thorough study of the experience we know as guilt. I took out my Bible and some biblical study tools and looked up the three Greek words translated "guilt" in our English versions. Much to my amazement, I found that none of these words refers to the emotion we know as guilt. One of the Greek words, *hupodikos*, means to be liable to judgment or punishment. Another, *opheilō*, means to owe or to be indebted. And the third, *enochos*, means to be liable, answerable, or deserving of death. Not one of these words refers to the emotional experience of psychological guilt. So I began to understand that guilt in the New Testament is a legal or judicial concept, not a feeling or experience.

I was shocked when I realized this fact. *Could it be*, I thought, *that for all these years I've had a distorted view of guilt? Could it be that God doesn't even want us to feel guilty?* These questions spurred my thinking and made me clarify my understanding of the biblical use of guilt and conscience.

I soon understood that many of us have a major problem in Christian living because we believe that God is the author of guilt feelings. Although these feelings make us painfully aware of our misdeeds, they don't really promote our growth. In fact, guilt feelings do more to frustrate and defeat us than anything else. When we begin to feel guilty and depressed, we soon are of little value to the work of God. When we feel like a failure, we are in no mood to tell others of our faith in Christ or to become enthusiastically involved in His work. We may drag along and carry out our obligations and responsibilities, but we really gain little enjoyment through our Christian life or service. Both our inner fulfillment and our involvement in Christian ministry suffer from the consequences of guilt.

Types of Guilt

Faced with all these negative results, it is amazing how consistently the church has taught that guilt feelings experienced by God's children come from God. I believe the reason the church has equated guilt feelings with the voice of God is due to its failure to distinguish between three different types of guilt and God's method of dealing with Christians and non-Christians. A brief look at these distinctions will help clarify the problem.

The first, *civil or legal guilt*, signifies the violation of a human law. It is a condition or state rather than a feeling or emotion. We can be guilty of breaking the speed limit, for example, even though we may not feel guilty.

Theological guilt, on the other hand, refers to the violation of divine standards or divine law. The Bible indicates that each of us is theologically guilty; we have all "sinned and fall short of the glory of God" (Rom. 3:23). But theological guilt is not a feeling or emotion. It is a condition or state of being in which we are less perfect than God intends us to be, but it is not necessarily accompanied by the emotional aspects of guilt. In a biblical sense, we are all in a continual state of theological guilt. There is never a moment when we are entirely free from sin, able to be the people God intends us to be. But this doesn't mean that we all *feel* guilty.

Psychological guilt is the punitive, painful, emotional experience that we commonly call guilt. In contrast to the legal and theological types of guilt, psychological guilt *is* an emotional feeling.

A lot of confusion arises from the misuse of these words. If we equate psychological guilt with theological guilt, every time the Bible says we are guilty (have sinned theologically), we will assume that we are being told to feel guilty. But this is incorrect. There is not a passage in the New Testament that commands a child of God to feel guilty.

Reactions to Guilt

Guilt produces one of four reactions.[1] Let's say people come up to you and say, "You're a lousy, miserable sinner." They berate you, threaten to reject you, and in general let you know they think you're a mess. In other words, they make you feel immensely guilty. Your natural reaction to this guilt might be to give up and agree with their negative evaluation. You may think to yourself, *They're right. I really am a mess.* By agreeing with their evaluation, you participate in their condemnation of yourself.

Some people, however, don't quickly give in to others' condemnation. In fact, as soon as they are made to feel guilty, they rebel. Someone might tell them, "You're a failure." Their response would be to think, *You haven't seen anything yet!* And they would start to make things worse. They're like a minister's son who told me how frequently he rebelled against his father and the church. During one counseling session, he gleefully told me how, during a drinking spree with some of his buddies, he lifted a bottle of beer to his lips and yelled, "Here's one for the deacon's board!"

Many people have had a similar experience. They attend church and try to obey biblical standards, but when they fall short, they feel guilty. Time after time, they work hard to try to be "good." But after each failure, they feel more guilty. Finally they just give up. They decide, *If I can't beat it* [sin], *I might as well join it!*

Others don't rebel so openly. They continue to give verbal assent to the Christian faith, but fail to get involved. They are routinely late, constantly preoccupied, or just not interested. They are much like a married person who is passively resistant. Responding to their mate's threats, nagging, or attempts to raise guilt, the husband or wife fights back with passivity. He or she fails to get ready on time, lets household tasks go undone, or gets involved in activities that neglect the family. Unfortunately, such passive rebellion stirs up more anger and guilt and compounds the problem.

What most of us don't realize is that these are normal reactions to guilt feelings. We should expect guilt to stir up rebellion. This is what the New Testament teaches. Paul writes, "The law was added so that the trespass might increase. But where sin increased, grace increased all the more" (Rom. 5:20). The Amplified Bible translates this verse: "But then Law came in, [only] to expand *and* increase the trespass [making it more apparent and exciting opposition]. But where sin increased *and* abounded, grace (God's unmerited favor) has surpassed it *and* increased the more *and* superabounded."

One purpose of the law of Moses, which contained threats of punishment and associated guilt feelings, was to make people sin more. The law was like a "Wet Paint Do Not Touch" sign. Man's immediate response was to reach out and touch, just to find out for himself. God knows that man is inwardly rebellious even when he doesn't recognize it, and the law exposes this by stimulating outward acts. This doesn't mean that the law creates rebellion; it seizes the dormant rebellion and brings it into the open so that we can realize its presence. Guilt does exactly the same thing; it also stirs up attitudes of rebellion.

The third way we react to guilt feelings is to deny them by rationalizing away our failures and our sins. We say things like: "Compared to other people, I'm not so bad." "That's just the way I am" or "That's just human nature." After Adam sinned and God confronted him in the Garden of Eden, what was his first response for plunging the human race into sin? "The woman whom *Thou* gavest to be with me," Adam said, "*she* [italics added] gave me from the tree, and I ate" (Gen. 3:12). In other words, Adam was saying, "God, the reason I went wrong was Eve. Since You gave me Eve, it's all Your fault."

Sometimes we hide our guilt by projecting our sins onto others. We find in them the sins and weaknesses we are hiding in ourselves. By focusing on others, we avoid becoming aware of our failures.

King David is a good example of this type of defense. He saw a beautiful woman named Bathsheba bathing on the rooftop. He called for her, committed adultery with her, and sent her husband, Uriah, to the front lines of battle so that he would be killed. The Lord then sent the prophet Nathan to convict David of his sin. Nathan said:

> There were two men in one city, the one rich and the other poor. The rich man had a great many flocks and herds. But the poor man had nothing except one little ewe lamb which he bought and nourished; and it grew up together with him and his children. It would eat of his bread and drink of his cup and lie in his bosom, and was like a daughter to him. Now a traveler came to the rich man, and he was unwilling to take from his own flock or his own herd, to prepare for the wayfarer who had come to him; rather he took the poor man's ewe lamb and prepared it for the man who had come to him (2 Sam. 12:1-4).

After David heard this, he became very angry and declared, "As the LORD lives, surely the man who has done this deserves to die."

Then Nathan said, "You are the man!"

You can imagine David's shock. He thought he was righteously passing judgment on a rich man who had taken a poor man's only lamb. He felt righteously indignant as long as he focused on another man's sin. But he was actually hiding his own sin. It is a strange paradox that the things we dislike in others are frequently the things we are unaware of in our own lives.

Unfortunately, the propensity for blaming others for our faults didn't die with Adam or David. We all do this continually. We argue with our mates, declaring our innocence and placing the blame on them. We do poorly at school and blame the professor. We get fired because "the boss is impossible." Each time we respond like this, we are denying our own responsibilities and failings because we are afraid of our guilt feelings. Since guilt attacks our self-esteem, we try to hide our failures.

Confession is the fourth typical reaction to guilt. Whenever we feel guilty, we like ourselves less, feel a sense of alienation from God, and fear His punishment or retribution. Therefore, we learn to admit that we're wrong in order to get relief. We ask forgiveness to overcome our psychic suffering. At first glance, this seems like a positive solution. Confession works like a magic wand; in no time at all, our guilt feelings vanish and we feel better about ourselves, accepted by God, and free from punishment.

But what about the motives for our confession? Were we really concerned about the person we hurt? Were we sorry about doing wrong, or were we just trying to rid ourselves of unpleasant guilt feelings? I must admit that through much of my life I confessed my sins more to relieve the pangs of guilt than to alter my behavior for the good of others. When this happens, we aren't really experiencing biblical repentance.

The Old Testament tells us of an Egyptian pharaoh caught up in a selfish confession. When the Israelite slaves pleaded to emigrate from Egypt, Pharaoh refused. Then God began to work miracles. The drinking water turned into blood; plagues of gnats, boils, and hail afflicted the nation. Chastened, Pharaoh sent for Moses and said, "I have sinned this time; the LORD is the righteous one, and I and my people are the wicked ones. Make supplication to the LORD, for there has been enough of God's thunder and hail; and I will let you go, and you shall stay no longer" (Exod. 9:27-28).

Sounds genuine, doesn't it? But as soon as the plagues stopped, Pharaoh's attitude changed. He wouldn't let the Israelites go. He hadn't really repented; he just wanted relief. Like many people who get caught, he was sorry—but not for his misdeeds. He was only sorry for the painful consequences of his misbehavior.

This kind of confession is based on a response we carry over from childhood. As children, we often said "I'm sorry" because we had been caught. As adults, we do a similar thing with God. Since we fear punishment, we quickly say, "I'm sorry." But our confession is much like a child caught with his hand in the cookie jar. We don't want God to "spank" us, so we say that we're sorry. Maybe we feel so depressed and sinful that we cannot sleep; so we confess our faults to clear our conscience. Feeling relieved, we then go to sleep. But we have not really changed our basic attitude and the next day our lives will not be any different.

These points lead us to the conclusion that guilt doesn't help us change our attitudes about ourselves. The following chart illustrates this point. We are naturally sinful and imperfect and consequently are led to commit wrong thoughts and actions. Then our rebellious actions trigger a fear of punishment, a lowered self-evaluation, or a fear of rejection. In response to this, we either: (1) give in and suffer depression and feelings of worthlessness; (2) rebel and fight back by committing even more wrongs; (3) deny we did any wrong and put the blame on someone else; or (4) superficially acknowledge our faults to get rid of the pain, but feel no genuine desire to change.

Reactions

Giving in to Accusations and Guilt	Rebelling	Rationalizing Away Our Sins	Superficial Confession

Feelings of Guilt

Fear of Punishment	Feelings of Rejection	Lowered Self-esteem

Specific Sinful Acts or Thoughts

Sinful Disposition

Christ Has Removed Our Guilt

Many of us Christians continue to feel guilty, in spite of the fact that when Christ died on the cross two thousand years ago, He paid the full penalty for all our sins. Jesus Himself said, "Whoever hears my word and believes him who sent me has eternal life and will not be condemned; he has crossed over from death to life" (John 5:24). In his letter to the Roman church, the apostle Paul said, "Therefore, there is now no condemnation for those who are in Christ Jesus" (Rom. 8:1). At the moment Jesus died on the cross, He paid the penalty for our sins once and for all. Although we may still *feel* like we deserve punishment for our misdeeds, we don't. He has fully paid for our past sins, our present sins, and even the ones that we haven't thought up yet! Although fears of punishment and rejection have a valid place in the life of the non-Christian who has not appropriated Christ's payment, they have no place in a Christian's life. Although God makes us aware of our sins (convicts us), we must be careful not to equate this process with the experience of guilt.

When the Bible speaks of conviction, it does not refer to guilty feelings. The Greek word *elenchō*, translated "conviction" in our English versions of the Bible, literally means "to bring to light" or "to bring to awareness." Conviction is the process of God bringing our weaknesses, failures, or inadequacies to our attention. It is not an oppressive emotional burden that God lays on us.

To help clarify the differences between conviction and the emotion of guilt, let's say that a friend points out an area of your life that needs strengthening. He brings to your awareness a need or weakness you have. This is the process of conviction. Once you are aware of the problem, you can react in one of several ways. You can say, "Yes, you certainly are right. I do have that problem and it's terrible. I'm really a louse for being that way and I really ought to change." You can respond to your friend's conviction with guilt and self-debasement.

You can also respond to the friend's statement by saying, "It's none of your business how I live, and besides, I'm no worse than the next guy!" You can become angry and rationalize your problems.

Yet, there is a third option. You don't have to respond in either of these ways. Thankful your friend has pointed out a need, you can be grateful and say, "Thanks, that really is a problem. I appreciate your interest and I'll try to work on that." You can respond with a constructive form of sorrow or regret without depreciating yourself. You can acknowledge your need without condemning yourself.

None of these reactions are the voice of God. They are our human response to the awareness of our failures. We all bring a history of experiences and attitudes to present-day encounters with the Lord. When we are convicted, we respond with whatever thoughts and feelings are lying in our personality. If we are prone to guilt and condemnation, we respond with self-inflicted mental punishment. But if we have learned to love and respect ourselves, we can respond to conviction in a positive and loving way.

Now let's bring this all together. Whenever we fall short of the expectations of our ideal self, our conscience triggers an awareness of our failure. (Actually, we are always aware of being less than we would like or could be.) This awareness in turn sets off some type of corrective response. If our minds have been programmed to threaten or accuse, we respond with feelings of guilt and condemnation. Our punitive self takes over and causes self-rejection and condemnation. It says that we are unacceptable or unlovable because we aren't good enough to avoid failure. If, on the other hand, our minds have been trained to lovingly acknowledge our failures, our loving corrective self will stimulate us toward a constructive type of regret. Within this perspective, we can feel bad about our sins and failures, but do not have to berate or condemn ourselves through guilt.

In summary, *our lack of self-love comes from an ever-present gap between what we are and what we want or think we should be* and from our self-rejection over the awareness of this gap. Try as we might, we never quite silence the awareness of our failures. Because we can't, we are never fully satisfied with ourselves and our performance. Just like Adam and Eve, our sins cause us to be afraid, guilty, and ashamed. Their sin created a split within the human personality that will never be completely healed. And this split is the source of our lack of self-love. Until that gap is somehow resolved, we can never fully love ourselves.

Antidotes to Guilt

Since the time of Adam, we have all tried a variety of ways to overcome the inner division and lack of self-acceptance that come from being less than we want or know that we should be. Some of us try to solve these problems by lowering our standards. We assume that by lowering our expectations, we will have a better chance of satisfying our inner expectations and therefore be better able to accept ourselves and avoid guilt. Sometimes this belief has merit. To the degree that we have set unrealistic, perfectionistic, or grandiose goals, we need to accept our human limitations and get on with life. But altering our standards can also lead to problems. To begin with, some of our expectations are divine, given us by God. If we try to lower these standards, we only set ourselves up for more frustration. This approach also fails because we can never block out all of our ideals or lower them to the point where we can always meet them.

A second way to minimize the effect of guilt and our lack of self-acceptance is to increase our performance. If we can't lower our expectations to meet our performance, then perhaps we can elevate our performance to a level that will prove acceptable. Although this sounds like the Christian thing to do, it is doomed to failure and is actually straight from the pit of hell. The Bible says, "The person who keeps every law of God, but makes one little slip, is just as guilty as the person who has broken every law there is" (James 2:10 LB). No matter how well we do or how mature we become, there is no way we can bridge the gap between our expectations and our performance. The Bible does not say that we merit self-acceptance and respect by improving our performance. There is only one way that gap is bridged—through Christ's sacrifice for our sins.

As we have seen, when Christ died on the cross, He once and for all settled the problem of our guilt and inner alienation. He acknowledged our utter inability to live up to either our own or God's desires; He also provided an alternative solution. He said that we would no longer have to strive so hard to gain a measure of acceptance. He said that all our sins are blotted out and that we are immediately made totally acceptable to God (see Ephesians 1:6). In other words, Christ not only bridged the gap between God's holiness and man's sinfulness; He also bridged the gap between our own demands and our actual performance.

Just as Christ provided the grounds for our acceptance by God, He also provided the grounds for our acceptance of ourselves.

And He is the only One who can resolve our lack of self-acceptance. Lowered standards or improved performance may temporarily placate our inner condemnation, but only the finished work of Christ can make us at ease with ourselves and our limitations. If God can accept us, surely we can learn to love ourselves. If God can forgive us, we can forgive ourselves. That's why guilt feelings should have no place in the Christian life. God is not the author of guilt feelings in the Christian. In fact, the Bible says that Satan is "the accuser of our brothers" (Rev. 12:10). He delights in causing us to question our forgiveness. As Christians we should be sensitive to our sins and respond to God's conviction with a loving, constructive regret or sorrow. But this constructive sorrow is not the same as guilt. Guilt is essentially a punitive process designed to mentally punish ourselves for our misdeeds. As such, it is inconsistent with the fact that the punishment for our sins has already been handled by Christ. Instead of responding to our sins and failures with guilt and self-punishment we should respond with a love-motivated, non-rejecting desire to change.

Guilt and Self-atonement

You may be thinking, *I realize that Christ has totally solved my guilt dilemma, but why do I so often still feel guilty? If guilt feelings do not come from God, why are they so difficult to overcome?*

The answer is twofold. We still experience guilt because we have been trained to feel guilty when we fail; we also feel guilty because we have a deep desire to satisfy our guilty conscience on our own. In other words, sometimes we feel guilty because of the psychic remnants of our past. Our parents taught us to feel guilty and we haven't overcome the habit. But we also feel guilty because we are trying to solve our sin problems by ourselves. Guilt, you see, is essentially a self-inflicted punishment.

When a Christian experiences guilt, he is really saying that he can either do something to make up for his sin, or at least cause himself to suffer for it. Even though he knows he lacks sufficient righteousness to merit God's acceptance, he assumes that

Christ's death on the cross was not totally sufficient for his sin. He feels a need to pay some more through self-inflicted guilt.

The Guilt Solution

How do we overcome guilt? We must practically apply the knowledge that our guilty condition has already been taken care of. Our sins have been totally paid for and forgiven. God is not the author of guilt in the Christian life. Christ is the One who justifies us, not the One who condemns (Rom. 8:33). We must acknowledge the fact that we can never succeed enough to be satisfied with ourselves; we must see ourselves the way Christ sees us. We must learn to rest in the assurance that Christ has made us totally acceptable. Then, once we know that we are totally acceptable to God, we can relax and stop trying to merit either His approval or our own. We can accept ourselves the way we are and go ahead with life. We can focus on the future and our growth, rather than on our past and our mistakes. We can begin each day with the assurance that whatever we may do, God will not make us feel guilty. He loves us and desires our best, and any corrections He portions out come from His heart of love.

Notes

1. This section is adapted from *Freedom From Guilt,* Bruce Narramore and Bill Counts (Santa Ana, Calif.: Vision House, 1974).

Self-love,
Sovereignty,
and
Surrender

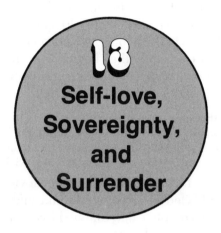

13
Self-love, Sovereignty, and Surrender

In the first twelve chapters, we have viewed different aspects of the biblical view of self-love and self-esteem. We have seen both the basis of our self-esteem in Creation and the undermining of self-esteem that comes through our own and others' sin. And we have seen God's provisions for the rebirth of self-esteem through the process of redemption. Underlying each of these discussions is the essential but still unnamed foundation of God's sovereignty.

Self-love and Sovereignty

Sovereignty is a little-used word today, but it is a key to understanding our relationship to God. What we believe about the sovereignty of God directly affects our attitude toward ourselves.

Explained simply, the sovereignty of God means that God is God. It means that He is the supreme being of the universe, absolutely powerful (Dan. 4:35), absolutely holy (Isa. 57:15), and absolutely wise (Ps. 104:24). The Bible describes it this way:

> Thine, O LORD, is the greatness and the power and the glory
> and the victory and the majesty, indeed everything that is in
> the heavens and the earth; Thine is the dominion, O LORD,
> and Thou dost exalt Thyself as head over all (1 Chron. 29:11).

The sovereignty of God also means that when we seek to understand our lives, we must begin with God. Any other focus is doomed to failure. There are only two perspectives on all of life. One begins with God; the other begins with man. If we begin with God, we end up with a certain world view. If we begin with man, we end up with another. Isaiah writes:

> "For My thoughts are not your thoughts, neither are your
> ways My ways," declares the LORD. "For as the heavens are
> higher than the earth, so are My ways higher than your ways,
> and My thoughts than your thoughts" (Isa. 55:8-9).

In other words, Isaiah tells us that a human viewpoint is finite and limited, while God's viewpoint is infinite and unlimited. Our perceptions are incomplete and dimmed by human understanding. Often we can see only one side of an issue, or we miss its meaning altogether. God's perceptions, on the other hand, are totally accurate and complete. They miss nothing and bring the entire picture into view.

Let's apply this principle to the concept of self-esteem. When we rely on our human viewpoint, we assume that self-respect and dignity must be earned. We assume that we must meet certain standards and that we have the capabilities necessary to reach them. In short, there are things we must *do* in order to be accepted. Our self-esteem is relative to our performance and to our own and others' estimation of us. As we have seen, this assumption often causes our lack of self-esteem. It leaves us struggling to accept ourselves and susceptible to feelings of guilt and self-debasement.

We bring these conditions on ourselves because we have taken on the role of God (or assigned that role to others). *We* have decided that self-esteem is earned. *We* have set up the standards (or accepted others' standards), and *we* have passed out punishment or reward. In every instance, we have taken on a responsibility that God reserved for Himself. We are much like Adam and Eve, who decided that they knew better than God what was best for them. They thought they would gain by taking matters into their own hands. And we do too. We think it is entirely reasonable to expect certain things from ourselves and condemn ourselves when we fall short. But this isn't God's perspective.

God knows that no one can ever have a truly positive and secure self-image unless it is based on a foundation other than our own. So, in His sovereignty, God established that foundation through His actions in creation, redemption, and revelation.

In creation, God pronounced us good (Gen. 1:31). Quite apart from our performance, He assigned a value to us. As we have seen, this is the one absolutely secure foundation for self-acceptance. When we deny our value, we are actually denying God's sovereignty. In essence, we are saying, "God, even though You are the Ruler and Creator of the universe, You don't know what You are talking about when You say that I am significant, valuable, and loved. You may be just, You may be all-powerful, and You may be completely wise, but in my case You are wrong!"

Although this statement sounds ridiculous, it exactly parallels our reasoning. We reject the sovereignty and wisdom of God regarding our value and esteem, and we set ourselves up as judges in His place.

The same paradox is true in the area of guilt and God's forgiveness. The Bible says, "Therefore, there is now no condemnation for those who are in Christ Jesus" (Rom. 8:1). However, we say, "We're terrible." The Bible says, "As far as the east is from the west, so far has He removed our transgressions from us" (Ps. 103:12). Yet we say, "We're guilty." The Bible says, "Jesus Christ, who gave himself for us to redeem us from all wickedness . . ." (Titus 2:14). But we say, "We must suffer more," rejecting the full meaning of our redemption and Christ's substitutionary death. In their place, we put our own perceptions. We exalt our reasoning above God's. We act as if we are sovereign. In the process, we are also rejecting God's sovereignty in revelation. When we demean or underestimate ourselves and continue to punish ourselves through guilt, we are saying that God's revelation about the worth of man and His forgiveness are not true when applied to us.

Since the results of operating from our human viewpoint and

rejecting God's sovereignty are painful, we usually do not see that this involves pride and the rejection of God's Word. We assume that self-rejection or self-punishment is actually humility, or at least acceptable—if not desirable. But if we take a closer look, we will recognize that this isn't so. By condemning ourselves, we are saying that Christ's payment for our sins was not sufficient. We are actually denying the adequacy of Christ's death and saying that His sacrifice is not enough for us.

The same principle is true in every aspect of our self-acceptance. We can either apply God's assessment of our worth to our lives, or substitute the evaluations of our parents, our mates, our acquaintances, or ourselves in its place. We can either apply God's revelation of forgiveness to our lives, or continue to punish ourselves and seek retribution. We can either accept God's standards of acceptance (Christ's imputed righteousness), or keep working toward our own.

Whatever our method, as long as we substitute our standards and our reasonings in place of God's, we are doomed to have problems with self-acceptance. It is just not possible for us to have a secure identity and a deep sense of personal worth until we accept the facts about us outlined in Scripture. But as soon as we understand and believe what Scripture says about us, we find a rich and enduring basis of self-acceptance.

At this point, I want to add a word of caution. If you are prone to feelings of guilt and condemnation, this concept may make you feel even more guilty. You may think, *Oh, no. On top of everything else, now I'm rejecting Christ's atonement!* This is a natural reaction for people who are especially susceptible to guilt. When they hear a truth, they immediately evaluate themselves by it. Let me encourage you to take it easy on yourself. It takes a while to learn to experience God's forgiveness. If you have years of experience condemning and criticizing yourself, you probably won't get rid of these emotions overnight. But you can intellectually acknowledge that your sins have already been taken care of and begin to grow into the fuller experience of God's forgiveness. Through an increased understanding of God's love for you and positive growth experiences with other Christians, you can learn to love yourself.

Self-love and Surrender

Some Christians speak a great deal about the concept of surrender. By this they mean that dedicated Christian commitment involves a total surrender of themselves to God. For years, this concept bothered me. In my mind, surrender conjured up pictures of defeat and capture. When an army surrenders, they have lost the battle. When a criminal surrenders, he is on his way to prison. And when a Christian surrenders, I had similar visions of some kind of defeat or loss.

Now I see the concept of surrender in a different light. The biblical concept of surrender has nothing to do with defeat. The act of surrender simply means to acknowledge the sovereignty of God and decide to live according to the pattern He has laid out for us in Scripture. If we are going to live life to the fullest and become all that God intends us to be, we must stop playing God and be willing to admit that our human reason and plans are not infallible. We must also admit that we cannot function at our best apart from God and must be willing to learn to look at life from God's perspective.

The child who is not content with being a child and is constantly obsessed with growing up and becoming his own boss is robbing himself of the enjoyment of his youth. Similarly, the Christian who keeps setting his own goals and expecting too much from himself—not accepting the fact that he is a person with significant limitations—robs himself of true fulfillment.

Recently, a Christian businessman who was extremely active in his church said, "For years, I've played God to myself and never knew it. I was as dedicated a Christian as you could be. But I could never accept myself the way I was. I always had to be more. I always lived with pressure and I couldn't really forgive myself. When it finally hit me that I was trying to play God and that I could learn to be myself and take it easy, I couldn't comprehend it. I just sat down, exhausted. Then, for the first time in years, I really started to relax. I felt at peace with myself. It was like a burden lifted. I thought, *I can just be me. God takes me the way I am!* It's a real relief now, not having to be God. I am easier on myself, my children, and my wife."

This man saw the futility of playing God. Although he was exceedingly productive, he was really not fulfilled and was constantly under pressure. Once he saw what he was doing, he started to relax. Much like a child who was secure in his parents' love, he could allow himself to relax and enjoy life.

Surrender to God is surrender to creative love. It is surrender of our lifelong desires to act or be someone we are not designed to be. Surrender means becoming all we are meant to be as we learn to accept our position under God. This healthy perspective allows us to give up both our superiority and inferiority. It allows us to give up self-hate and self-debasement and even allows us to give up many of our frustrations. Since we no longer need to work to impress others or to hide our weaknesses and fears once we allow God to be God, we can admit that we all have failed and that we are all equal members of mankind. E. Stanley Jones states:

> When you surrender to Christ, all self hate, all self loathing, all self rejection drop away. How can you hate what He loves? How can you reject what He accepts? How can you look down on what He died for? You are no longer a person, you are "a person for whom Christ died." If He died for me, there must be something in me worth dying for. So surrender to Christ saves you, on the one hand, from self assertion, always wanting to occupy the center of attention, and, on the other hand, from shyness which is always shrinking and thinking, "what do they think of me?" . . . You are not a worm, nor a wonder. You are the ordinary becoming the extraordinary, all due to Him. So you can be yourself because you are His self. You are free to be.[1]

Sovereignty and surrender—two words in the Christian vocabulary that speak of our commitment to God and others. But they also speak to the question of self-fulfillment. As we accept God's sovereignty, we reap the benefits of increasing self-regard, self-awareness, and self-acceptance. And as we surrender to His will for us, we find ourselves in harmony with the Creator of the universe and the human personality. We become free to grow, actualize, and develop into all we are meant to be.

Notes

1. E. Stanley Jones, *Victory Through Surrender* (Nashville: Abingdon Press, 1966), pp. 45-46.

Partners
in
Self-esteem

14
Partners in Self-esteem

Love is a response attitude and emotion that we develop in the course of life. The newborn infant has no love. He doesn't even know that others exist. Only as his bodily apparatus matures and his personality develops will he learn to love. And even then, he will only learn to love if others love him first.

No thinking person would suggest an infant is born with love, since love requires an awareness and appreciation of others that is absent in his early days of life. But it is just as obvious that infants have a capacity to learn to love. In their intimate relationships with parents, infants gradually learn to understand the experience of love. They find out what it's like to be cared for, to be looked after, to be valued and esteemed. As they experience this love, they soon begin to love in turn. They begin to value and appreciate the efforts of others and start to reach out to them.

As adults, we sometimes forget that love is learned. So we say to another person; "I don't love my mate enough"; or "I don't love God enough"; or "I don't love myself." We assume that we need to love in a deeper way. In a sense, our diagnosis is correct. We may be lacking love. But in another sense, we're wrong. Since love is a response, we cannot love until we first experience love. When we believe that we don't have sufficient love for others we probably aren't receiving sufficient love ourselves.

People have told me, "I don't love God enough." I frequently reply, "No, that's not your trouble. Your trouble is that you don't know how much God loves you." Then I point out that love is not something we conjure up through effort, positive thinking, or even prayer. Love for ourselves, God, and others is a response to being loved. The apostle John clearly spells this out when he writes, "We love because he first loved us" (1 John 4:19). John doesn't say that we love God because we should, or because we are instructed to, but because He loved us first. What's true of our relationship with God is true of our relationship with ourselves and others. There is no way we can stir up feelings of respect and love apart from being loved. Self-love cannot take place in a vacuum any more than we can love others while in isolation.

Have you ever stopped to think why God instructed us to love each other? I mean *really* stopped to think? I know we all think love is a Christian virtue, but why is love so overwhelmingly important? Christ tells us love is essential because it is the mark of a real Christian. "By this all men will know that you are My disciples, if you have love for one another" (John 13:35 NASB).

I am convinced that one reason God instructs us to love each other is to communicate a sense of value to each other. God's very nature is to love. He created us, He loves us, He values us, and He expects us to return that love to each other. Jesus said:

> As the Father has loved me, so have I loved you. Now remain in my love. If you obey my commands, you will remain in my love, just as I have obeyed my Father's commands and remain in his love. I have told you this so that my joy may be in you and that your joy may be complete. My command is this: Love each other as I have loved you (John 15:9-12).

Just as Christ's love for us demonstrates our significance to Him, our love for other persons communicates esteem for them.

Most of us are used to looking at only one end of the process of loving others. We focus on our need to love and on Christ's instructions for us to love, but usually don't give a lot of thought to being loved. How many sermons have you heard on the virtue of being loved or allowing others to love you? Don't most sermon topics deal with what we should do for others? Let's give attention to the other side of the process. If God tells us to love each other, it must be because there are positive results in loving others. In other words, the purpose of our love is to show others that they are important, significant, and valuable. Without our love, they will never know their worth. God uses parents, children, mates, and friends to communicate His love to others.

Now let's change places with the person we are loving. If no one loves us, how will we ever know our value and significance? If we are to have that attitude toward ourselves, we must be esteemed and valued. This means we can never have a positive self-image apart from other people. In our early life, we cannot know love unless our parents love us. And as we grow older, we continue to need to have other people love us and thereby demonstrate God's love for us. This is one of the major reasons God instructs us to love each other.

This has far-reaching implications. If we want to learn to love ourselves, we must first let others love us. We can't learn to love ourselves in isolation, and Scripture memorization won't solve problems stemming from a lack of self-acceptance. Although the foundation of self-esteem is found in the biblical truths of creation and redemption, we need the help of others as we learn to accept ourselves. This is why the Bible tells us to encourage one another (Heb. 10:25), bear burdens for one another (Gal. 6:2), and confess our sins to one another (James 5:16).

A healing process takes place when we are loved by others. Our attitude of self-rejection developed from our relationship with parents and other significant people. At that time, we learned to expect criticism and pressure and to experience guilt and condemnation. Our parents, bothered by their own difficulties in accepting themselves and others, at times undermined our self-esteem. They were not fully successful in communicating our significance and were not able to fully demonstrate God's unconditional love and complete forgiveness. Because of their failures and our desire for perfection, we entered adulthood with less than an adequate evaluation of ourselves.

Friends can help us break out of these patterns of condemnation and rejection. By listening to us—even in times of failure—they let us know that we don't have to perform successfully in order to be loved. They help us to experience that we don't have to be punished in order to gain the motivation to improve. Their understanding tells us, "We all have struggles and frustrations. We all get down on ourselves at times and we all feel like a failure on occasion. But we understand and love you just the same. We also know that God accepts you just the way you are."

Biblical relationships generate healing. We all have areas of our life that we don't like. As we've seen, we try to hide these failures because we fear rejection or evaluation. But in doing so, we become deceitful. We act like someone we're not. We put on a front to impress others and gradually learn to hide our true self and our emotions. This retreat puts us under increased pressure. Not only do we have a problem or a weakness, but we have to expend a lot of effort keeping it secret. We begin to withdraw, lose our spontaneity, or try to overcompensate by magnificent performance. In every instance, we remove ourselves from honest sharing. No one really knows what's going on inside us.

Our lives don't have to be like that. All of us can begin to work on our relationships with others. In our heart, we long to be accepted, but we fear that honesty and closeness will only bring rejection. This is not the case. Once others know that we are human, they can drop their own facade and reach out even more. If you have difficulty building self-esteem, let me encourage you to open up to a few close friends. Let them know the way you feel and let them share with you. Some problems of self-acceptance are so deep that they need the help of a "professional friend"—a psychologist, counselor, or psychiatrist—but most of us can grow immensely through interaction with others. Sometimes the person is our mate; other times we share with a small group of people seeking Christian growth. But whatever the format, remember that self-love is a result of being loved. When we allow others to accept us, we become more open and accepting of ourselves. We see firsthand demonstrations of the nature of God's love and find a deeper understanding of His love for us. This is why Christ said, "Love each other as I have loved you" (John 15:12).

**A Final
Word**

15

A Final Word

One day during His earthly ministry, Jesus took Peter, James, and John up a mountain. As they stood together, Jesus was miraculously transformed. "His face shone like the sun, and his clothes became as white as the light" (Matt. 17:2). Then a bright cloud came over them and a voice said, "This is my Son, whom I love; with him I am well-pleased. Listen to him!" (Matt. 17:5). This transfiguration, or transformation, is one of the three times that writers of Holy Scripture use the Greek word *metamorphoō*, which literally means "transformed" or "changed." Paul also uses this concept in Romans 12:2 and 2 Corinthians 3:18. On these latter two occasions, the word is applied to those of us who have placed our faith in Jesus Christ. In Romans, Paul says that we should "not conform any longer to the pattern of this world, but be transformed by the renewing of your mind." In 2 Corinthians, he says, "And we, who with unveiled faces all reflect the Lord's glory, are being tranformed into his likeness with ever-increasing glory, which comes from the Lord, who is the Spirit." In both passages, Paul writes that we are all in a process of growth or transformation throughout our lives. The end result of that process is conformity to the image of God.

In two other passages, Paul writes of the same process:

> For those God foreknew he also predestined to be conformed to the likeness of his Son, that he might be the firstborn among many brothers. And those he predestined, he also called; those he called, he also justified; those he justified, he also glorified. What, then, shall we say in response to this? If God is for us, who can be against us? (Rom. 8:29-31).

Speaking of the new bodies that we will have in eternity, Paul writes:

> And just as we have borne the likeness of the earthly man, so we shall bear the likeness of the man from heaven (1 Cor. 15:49).

These passages from Paul's writings all mention our ultimate destination. They make it clear that when our lives on earth are over, everyone who has placed his faith in Christ will be restored to perfection. But they also tell us that we are already involved in this process of transformation. Created in the image of God, fallen into sin, and redeemed through Christ's death, we are now being restored to our original condition. Our image, marred by sin, is being renewed. In fact, God already considers us to be new persons. "Therefore, if anyone is in Christ, he is a new creation; the old has gone, the new has come!" (2 Cor. 5:17).

The moment we place our faith in Jesus Christ, we are changed. While we are not yet perfect, we are different. We are alive to spiritual principles, open to the voice of God, and actively involved in a process of total restoration. The end result of the process will be a return to the beauty we possessed when we came from the hand of God. We haven't arrived yet, but we are in the process. Paul said, "Brothers, I do not consider myself yet to have taken hold of it. But one thing I do: Forgetting what is behind and straining toward what is ahead, I press on toward the goal to win the prize for which God has called me heavenward in Christ Jesus" (Phil. 3:13-14).

This ongoing restoration comes through increased understanding of our areas of weakness, increased freedom from the bonds of guilt, increased understanding of Scripture, and increased intimacy with others. We are all at different stages along the road, but we can walk with equal confidence because, as Paul puts it, "being confident of this, that he who began a good work in you will carry it on to completion until the day of Christ Jesus" (Phil. 1:6).

When Christ returns and we reach our destination in eternity, we will be totally restored to our full and complete self. Jesus Christ Himself will "transform the body of our humble state into conformity with the body of His glory, by the exertion of the power that He has even to subject all things to Himself" (Phil. 3:21 NASB).

This truth is the basis of our self-esteem. Made in the image of God and in the process of being restored to that design, we are able to have a deep awareness of who we are. Although this life is exceedingly important, it is only one phase of our existence. At both ends, we find ourselves in a condition of complete perfection. We were created in God's image before we were born and will be transformed completely into His image after death. In the meantime, our current weaknesses and failures do not destroy the essence of our nature. We are the apex of God's creation, formed by His own hands and destined to spend eternity with Him. With this identity, how can we help but love ourselves? And with this identity, how can we help but love the One who made it possible?

Scripture Index